What Women Want When They Test Men

How to Decode Female Behavior, Pass a Woman's Tests, and Attract Women Through Authenticity

By Bruce Bryans

Legal Disclaimer

Although the information in this book may be very useful, it is sold with the understanding that neither the author nor the publisher is engaged in presenting specific psychological, emotional, or sexual advice. Nor is anything in this book intended to be a diagnosis, prescription, recommendation, or cure for any specific kind of psychological, emotional, or sexual problem. Each person has unique needs and this book cannot take these individual differences into account.

This book is copyright © 2015 by Bruce Bryans with all rights reserved.

It is illegal to copy, distribute, or create derivative works from this book in whole or in part or to contribute to the copying, distribution, or creating of derivative works of this book.

No part of this report may be reproduced or transmitted in any form whatsoever, electronic, or mechanical, including photocopying, recording, or by any informational storage or retrieval system without expressed written, dated and signed permission from the author.

ISBN-13:978-1515234043

ISBN-10:1515234045

Table of Contents

The Introduction _____ 1

CHAPTER 1: *Accepting the Ugly Truth* _____ 9

CHAPTER 2: *Why Women Test Men* _____ 21

CHAPTER 3: *How Women Test Men* _____ 33

CHAPTER 4: *Communicating with a Testing Woman* _____ 49

CHAPTER 5: *Be Your Own Man and Earn Her Respect* _____ 69

CHAPTER 6: *Being the Rock a Woman Needs* ___ 93

CHAPTER 7: *The Single Man and the Women That Test Him* _____ 119

CHAPTER 8: *Building a Better Man* _____ 141

The Conclusion _____ 161

The Introduction

Let's imagine three men if you will: Richard, Mark, and David.

Richard has no problem attracting women but he can't seem to manage a successful relationship to save his life. He would ultimately walk away from a relationship if a girlfriend became moody or unreasonable. Richard figures that the women he meets are all the same: too demanding, nagging, emotional, and disrespectful.

He becomes completely intolerant of the irrational nature of female behavior and decides to keep his relationships with women light and non-committal. He'd rather be single than deal with the mysterious wiles of a woman in a more intimate relationship. Richard is convinced that he's meant to be a perpetual bachelor.

Mark is a nice guy, a REALLY nice guy. He is *always* there for his buddies and would do anything to make his woman happy. Anything. He even lets his wife make most, if not all of the decisions. Mark is on his second marriage and it appears that his wife has lost all sexual attraction for him. She loves him, but she's not entirely sure she loves him enough to turn down a more "attractive" man.

She pushes Mark around with her demands and feels compelled to hassle him for no apparent reason. Mark really wants to be a good husband. So he tries not to upset her further by being unquestionably considerate with her. He is desperate to change things so he pursues her with spectacular gusto; meeting all of her needs, wants, wishes, and wanton desires with double the effort. His wife has grown even more contemptuous of him. She starts considering divorce.

David's been married to the same woman for several years and she's absolutely mad about him. David isn't the most romantic man on the planet but he does what he can to make his wife feel beautiful, special, desired, and loved.

He's a straight shooter. He speaks his mind, has strong personal boundaries, and doesn't care what people outside of his honor group thinks about him. He's especially honest with his wife and isn't afraid to "upset" her if he knows the truth will make her a better person or will improve their intimacy.

When she gets overly emotional, demanding, or unreasonable, David confidently weathers her storms, stands his ground, and loves her passionately with a stout heart. His wife trusts him one-hundred percent and she feels secure under his leadership. And most importantly, his wife is extremely responsive to him when it comes to sex. In other words, she just can't help herself around him.

Here are three different men, all of the same age and demographic, but with very different experiences with the opposite sex. What's going on here?

The main difference lies in how these men think and respond to a strange and sometimes misunderstood aspect of a woman's behavior: *the subconscious need to test a man to determine his capability to lead and capacity to love her.*

Millions…no, billions of men around the world have no idea that the women they know and love are testing them. These men go about their lives interacting with the opposite sex in absolute darkness, ignorant to the fact that they're being judged, appraised, approved, and rejected based on their subconscious reactions to female testing.

To make matters worse, most women have no idea that they test men either. Sure, you have some women who are so experienced in dealing with men that they know exactly how to test a man to get the results they're looking for. But for the majority of men and women, they have no idea that this sort of gender-based interaction is taking place whether they're conscious of it or not.

If you had no idea what women want when they test men, you're about to take a journey onto a road less traveled – the murkier side of feminine and masculine gender-dynamics. But be warned: you cannot unlearn what you read in this book, no matter how hard you try.

What Women Really Want When They Test Men

Whether it's a revealing conversation or an online dating profile, if you closely observe the language women use you'll find that they want to be with a man who can confidently take the lead and make decisions, has strong personal boundaries, and knows how to love her like…a man.

While different women want very different things there seems to be at least one particular *need* that pops up consistently. Women usually communicate this need in vague language that some men find confusing. This happens because when women do confess this need it appears counterintuitive to how most men were brought up to interact with women.

For example, here's a small sampling of confessions women have made that men have come across at one point or another:

- "I want a man who knows how to put me in my place."

- "He's the only guy to ever call me out when I get out of hand."

- "I like that he doesn't let me get away with everything."

- "I just wish he'd stand up to me sometimes. He's such a pushover."

- "He just lets me do whatever I want. It's like he doesn't have a backbone."

- "I just wish he'd do what he wants for a change. He lets me make all the decisions."

- "He's really honest with me. I don't always like it, but I know I can trust him."

A lot of men these days have difficulty accepting the truth that many women *prefer* to be with a man who isn't afraid to stand up to them, who challenges them, and who refuses to be pushed around when a woman (or anything else for that matter) tests him. This is especially true of women who seek a more traditional male-female gender dynamic in their romantic relationships.

While some women understand this and can confidently admit that they *need* a man who can handle them when they lose themselves in their emotions, others aren't as aware of this desire. Unfortunately, even when they are aware, there's a chance that they might be too embarrassed to even admit it.

Due to the various social constraints placed on female sexuality women tend to conceal what they are *really* attracted to in men. The reality of having an overwhelming sexual attraction to a highly assertive, strong-willed, and perhaps even dominant man might make a woman feel ashamed, especially in today's highly feminized and politically-correct society.

It's very RARE for a woman to admit that she's sexually attracted to a man who doesn't always give her what she wants, who speaks his mind, and who challenges her to be more authentic.

Who Should Read This Book?

This book is for the man who wants to "wear the pants" and keep them on as he relates to that beautiful yet perplexing specimen we call woman. If you're a man and you adhere to the idea of *taking the leadership role* as you date and relate with women, you will love this book. If you're a man and you'd rather the woman you're with *take the leadership role*, then this book is not for you.

The same goes for women. If you fancy the idea of being with a man who will confidently *take the leadership role* in a relationship with you, you too will love this book. On the other hand, if you believe that a woman should *take the leadership role* in the relationship, you will have no need for this book.

If you're a woman reading this book I implore you to not confuse gender "equality" with gender "uniformity." Although men and women were created equal they are inherently different. Therefore, their natural and most preferred *roles* in a relationship will be different. This book focuses on helping passive, unaware, or misinformed men to understand and accept these differences.

If you're a guy, there's a good chance that this book will challenge your way of thinking when it comes to dating and relating with women. I will not hold any punches but do know that by the end of this book you WILL have learned something that will make you far more attractive to a high-quality woman and far more skillful in dealing with her in a relationship. On the other hand, if you are a woman, there's a good chance that this book will make you re-evaluate the way you've been relating with the men in your life.

Generally speaking, if you're married or in a long-term relationship and the woman you love constantly nags you, creates drama, challenges you, belittles you, or manipulates you, it's time to reinforce your personal boundaries and pass her tests.

Some women would never admit this but what they want is a man who knows how to walk that thin line between caring, thoughtful lover and firm, assertive leader. The man who masters the art of being the perfect gentleman and strong alpha male is the ideal specimen to a quality woman.

So, if you've been leaning too hard on the side of the nice guy, you're about to be guided back towards balance. Prepare for a dramatic shift in your paradigm.

CHAPTER 1:

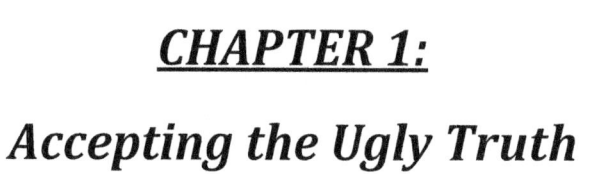

Accepting the Ugly Truth

A New Way to Look at Female Behavior

Things are going well with the woman in your life. You rarely argue, you really enjoy her company, and the sparks are flying in every direction between you two. Then all of a sudden, she explodes on you for something so incredibly outlandish that you can't help but wonder if you're being punk'd by Ashton Kutcher and his mischievous cohorts.

Her emotional blow up comes out of left field and catches you completely off guard. The more you try to explain yourself the worse it gets. The result? She slowly descends into a full emotional meltdown; fluctuating between irrational anger and hysterical crying while you feebly attempt to apologize to her for something you're no longer sure you're innocent of.

So what in the name of Davy Crockett is going here? Well, my friend, you just failed a woman's test. It's sad to say because you probably didn't have any idea that you were actually taking one. In an attempt to restore harmony once again you resort to endless apologies, a bouquet of "I'm sorry" flowers, and a solemn promise to "make things right again" even though you didn't do anything wrong in the first place.

Fail.

So what's a man to do? Well, the first step is to recognize what is really going on when women behave this way and secondly, learn how to approach these situations with the *mindset* of a mature, masculine man.

The Mature Approach – Changing the Way You Think

It's essential that men change their paradigms when it comes to dealing with a difficult, emotional, or demanding woman. The reason? A man can only take so much emotional abuse from a woman before he eventually breaks down or loses it altogether. That breaking point may come ten to twenty years later in a marriage or it may come a few months into a new relationship.

The fact is, being tested by a woman and not understanding what's *really* going on underneath the surface causes a man to experience deep-rooted feelings of anger, frustration, bitterness, and resentment – all the emotions that cause him to fall out of love and eventually despise a woman.

A man may find himself extremely demoralized over time if his woman constantly tests him and he doesn't know how to respond successfully. As he fails her tests, she begins to withhold her respect, support, and physical affection from him. Therefore, he begins to feel unloved, misunderstood, and disrespected. No matter how strong he thinks he is, over time his armor will crack until he starts feeling resentment and bitterness.

Sadly, once a man's feelings of bitterness towards his woman begin to overwhelm him he will move beyond simply despising the woman he once cared for. Instead he'll move into the most dangerous state of all – indifference. The man who is indifferent towards his woman doesn't care what happens to her or the relationship.

At this point, the poor guy has officially "checked out" of the relationship and is only one argument away from calling it quits. That is of course, if his equally frustrated wife or girlfriend hasn't already initiated her own exit strategy.

Unfortunately, some guys just don't know that women naturally test men. However, when they are tested they KNOW when they've said or done the "wrong" thing. It's a gut feeling men get when they know something's wrong but they don't have a clue as to what's going on and how they can possibly fix it.

It's like what Morpheus said in the film, *The Matrix*. It feels like a *"splinter in your mind."* You know you're failing something because she's unhappy, you're unhappy, and when you try to say or do something to fix it things only get worse.

This sort of thing happens a lot more often than men and women realize. And while it may be extremely agonizing for a woman to be with a man who constantly fails her tests, it is overwhelmingly painful for a man to feel as if nothing he does can make his woman happy.

When a man *interprets* a woman's testiness as being mean or emotionally abusive he will not respond in a way that leads to a harmonious solution. Instead, he habitually internalizes her tests as personal attacks and over time the damage to his self-esteem will be near insurmountable.

Even good guys who genuinely love their wives or girlfriends can reach the point of emotional coldness where they no longer feel *anything* for a woman. Consider this the next time you hear of a man divorcing his wife or breaking up with his girlfriend for "no apparent reason."

A major factor that causes some relationships to self-destruct for "no apparent reason" is because of a miscommunication; where a woman tests her man hoping that he'll man up and assert himself but instead he does the complete opposite and supplicates to her demands. The problem isn't that he's incapable of standing up for himself and standing up to her; the problem is a miscommunication due to a lack of understanding.

Why Every Man Needs to Know This

Guess what? You're being tested every single day of your life. Your boss will test you, your parents will test you, your friends will test you, your coworkers will test you, your employees will test you, your children will test you, and even your dog will test you just to see how much he can get away with before you put the smack down. The world is testing you, my friend, and there's nothing you can do to stop it.

However, the best thing for you to do is to learn how to deal with it when the tests come your way. Wishing the world were different is not only foolish, but a total waste of energy. Accepting that the world can be a mean, harsh, and judgmental place changes your paradigm and opens up your mind to learn how to deal with its conflicts and challenges.

As you already know, women will test you whether you like it or not. Women will test your strength and they will test your devotion. As a relationship matures and you learn how to lead and love a woman in the way she requires, the tests can die down. But when you lose your path, become indifferent, or your priorities shift away from her, the tests will begin and perhaps intensify.

Some guys (bless their hearts) have this erroneous idea that a woman who tests them isn't worth their time. They believe that a woman should just accept them for who they are and not have to qualify them. In their skewed view of the world, they believe that by being themselves women should have no need to test them, push their buttons, or create drama.

These poor chaps view the world how they *wish* women were instead of viewing the world *as it is*. Their maps don't match the territory, so the mere thought of having to deal with a woman's tests (especially since they're such wonderful, honest, "nice" guys) seems ridiculous.

Well, if you're one of these guys I suggest that you never date or get into a relationship with another woman ever again. Because no matter how you *wish* women were, you will be tested.

Guys who choose to reject the concept that women are testing them have a victim mentality. For them, the reality of how women think and act towards men is too harsh so they'd rather live a lie than embrace the truth like a man. They believe the world should bend to them rather than working on themselves to become the kind of men high-quality women can respect, love, and support.

It's even possible that men like this struggle with the idea of being dominant. They think being dominant is the same as being a dictator, and these limiting beliefs roadblock them from accepting all that women require from a strong, masculine man.

But in reality, men who enjoy lifelong, successful marriages and dating lives all have at least one thing in common: they figured out what women want in a man. Whether they learned from a mentor, a friend, a book, or through painful trial and error is irrelevant. What's most important is that they *accepted* the truth of what women want and they acted on that knowledge until they got the positive results they desired.

But Not All Women Test Men...Right?

Wrong. In fact, the opposite is true. The more a woman is interested or invested in you the more she will test you. It doesn't matter if she's your wonderful wife of twenty years or the sweet girl next door that you've been spying on. It doesn't even matter if she's considered low maintenance and supposedly drama-free. All women test men.

Now, like anything related to relationships there are no absolute absolutes. Some men may find themselves in situations in which women simply do not test them in any capacity. That's not necessarily a good thing, and here's why. The only women who won't test you *at all* are:

1. Women who have zero romantic interest in you, and...

2. Highly aggressive or experienced women who already have (and prefer) control over you.

Women test men because they seek both love and leadership from them. Therefore, if she has no romantic or emotional interest in you, you won't be tested. And if she's not interested in a relationship dynamic in which you lead her you probably won't be tested either.

As you can see, these are situations with women that I assume you'd rather not get into in the first place. So aside from those two situations any sort of romantic relationship with a woman who desires masculine leadership (the kind of woman you want) is going to be filled with tests, teasing, conflicts, and challenges.

Evolve or Suffer

Only men who learn to embrace life's challenges will reap its sweet rewards, especially when it comes to cultivating relationships with the fairer sex. And guess what? Women don't care if you really are a nice guy, who attends church regularly, has a good job, and is well-liked by his friends. What she's more concerned about on a deep, primal level is: *"Are you man enough to lead and love me?"* And the only way she can find that out is by testing you.

So be a man and deserve what you want. If you choose not to learn what women want and how they test men or you fail to figure it out on your own, you'll be doomed to a life of overwhelming challenges with women who will find themselves painfully dissatisfied with you. This is the hell-on-earth reserved for men who choose not to empathize with women.

On the other hand, learning how to relate to women on this level helps you to become a better, more integrated man. As you excel in this area you'll eventually find that women's tests have little to no effect on you. And as you learn to walk the thin line between being a powerful leader and an attentive lover you would have crossed over into unconscious competence.

This happens when your awareness of female behavior is so ingrained in your subconscious that you react without thinking about it. You're no longer *trying* to pass her tests because you act instinctively. At this point, you're a bona-fide Jedi when relating with your woman and there's very little she, or anyone else for that matter, can do to throw you off base. You've become the powerful man she can rely on as her tests prove that your behavior is congruent to what she needs.

This is all a part of the process of becoming a well-integrated, mature, masculine man. She won't need to test you as much because she knows that you "get it." But when and if her insecurities do flare up you'll be well equipped to deal with her…like a man. That, my friend, is why you need to know this.

Will Women Always Test Me?

Short answer: Yes. There's nothing you can do to control her tests. You cannot control when they happen and the nature in which you will experience them. That's just the way it is, so get used to the idea if you want to get along well with the opposite sex, especially in a long-term relationship or marriage.

When considering the frequency and volume of a woman's tests one must consider it within the context of *why* she's testing. Is she testing you for fun and personal gratification or is she testing you because she's insecure? With this question in mind, here's the rationale: The more secure a woman feels around you the *less* she's going to test you in order to gain reassurance of your congruence or commitment.

On the other hand, the more attraction a woman feels for you the *more* she's going to test you in order to experience playful displays of your masculinity. The latter is the kind of test that you WANT to experience with a woman, preferably often. The former is the kind of test you probably want a whole lot less of. This is the kind of test I'll be referring to for the rest of this section.

Now, from my personal experiences with women and from what I've observed from other men and their relationships, a woman's tests can be reduced or the negative emotions you experience from them can be diminished. This results from one of two situations:

1. You're playing your role well in your relationship, i.e., you are a mature, masculine man that leads and loves his woman unconditionally, or...

2. She's playing her role well, i.e., she is a mature, feminine woman who respects and supports her man unconditionally.

When both or either of these situations is not present, you may find yourself on the receiving end of a load of congruence or commitment tests that have the capacity to overwhelm you.

If you're playing your role well her experiences with you will ensure her of your leadership/loyalty and keep her insecurities at bay to a greater extent. When she's playing her role well she is far more likely to *exercise control over her emotions* and therefore submits to your masculine leadership to a greater extent.

If you're not being the MAN she *needs*, you're giving her female mind an excuse to conjure up ways to either affirm or suppress her insecurities – by testing you. If she's not being the supportive, submissive woman you love by respecting you unconditionally, again, her female mind starts to *feel* the power imbalance that will cause her to test you. If you're not playing your role and she's not playing hers all at once…well, let's just say you're in for the ride of your life buddy.

I mention this only to illustrate that a man cannot avoid being tested by a woman, but he can keep those tests in check by being the man she needs. Being the man she needs ensures that her insecurities are minimized and that your capacity to lead and love her cannot be reproached. Being the man she needs also ensures that when she does test you, you are less likely to experience her tests in a negative way.

Life Will Test You

From the moment you step out into the world, you're being tested; even more so as a man. There's nothing you can do to avoid being tested day in and day out. You'll either learn how to deal with it or you'll find yourself constantly failing life's tests.

I know this all sounds quite philosophical and perhaps even a bit esoteric, but believe me when I tell you that one of the most valuable qualities you can develop as a man is to learn how to remain *unmoved* by the various tests life throws at you. Getting a grip on your emotions and overcoming your fears will make you an unmovable rock when life throws a few storms at you. But we have to start somewhere, and what better place to start than when dealing with the opposite sex?

Because I wanted to make this book as logical and practical as possible I'm going to be blunt. If you want to remain steadfast not only as you relate with women but in other areas of your life, you must learn to embrace rejection and enjoy conflict. Read that last sentence again.

Now, I'm not saying that you need to have a hard on anytime you get into a confrontation, but having the mindset that says, "I can handle this!" in the midst of life's challenges will set you apart as the kind of man a woman can trust and therefore give herself to in full.

Learning not only how to deal with rejection and conflict but actively seeking them out will harden you. Real life experience is invaluable, and there's nothing like being out in the field for yourself, testing your own mettle against the tides and turns of this thing called life.

CHAPTER 2:

Why Women Test Men

Survival of the Fittest

For most women the act of testing men is a survival mechanism used for gaining vital information about a man's character. Because a woman craves security and a weak man poses great risk to the well-being of both her and her offspring, she's going to use various techniques, albeit unknowingly, to ensure that the man she's interested or invested in can be counted on now and in the future.

The scariest part about this kind of behavior that guys can't seem to accept is that for women, this process happens subconsciously. Most women don't know that they're doing it and the ones who do realize what's going on only recognize what they're doing AFTER they've tested a man. Just as it requires a ton of self-control to not stare at a half-naked woman in your field of vision, so it is with this habit of testing for women.

In my book, _What Women Want In A Man_, I stress the point that what women really want from men is the experience of desiring and being desired by a strong, confident man. Women who exude feminine grace prefer men who lead just as well as they love. You cannot have one without the other if you want to cultivate a successful relationship with a good woman. It's this insatiable quest for balance that compels a woman to keep a man on his toes in a relationship by testing him.

If a man becomes passive, a woman may instinctively challenge him in an attempt to make him assert himself. An example? Think of the husband who's been out of work for months on end. He may soon find that his wife has become less patient with him as she constantly challenges his authority in an attempt to pressure him to seek out provisions for the family.

On the other hand, if a man becomes far too dominating and self-involved, a woman may provide him with just enough drama in an attempt to draw out his more compassionate, caring side.

Think of the boyfriend who has grown slightly distant due to a big project at his job. He's not cheating or planning on leaving his girlfriend, but her survival mechanism kicks in and forces her to seek out reassurance. How? By throwing an emotional fit that gets his attention and compels him to prove that he's still committed to her and hasn't "checked out" of the relationship. Women require men to both lead and love them, and they'll pull out all the stops necessary to get these needs met.

What a Woman Gains from Testing You

Short answer: a TON of information. By testing a man, a woman gains access to an unsullied source of information that she wouldn't readily have access to if she had just asked him a few questions. What this means is that by testing you she can figure out what kind of man you really are without you having to verbalize it to her. Going this route allows her to bypass any misinformation that you may give her and get straight to the truth. When a woman tests you, you cannot hide what's inside.

A quick Internet search for the definition of a test reveals that: *a test is a procedure intended to establish the quality, performance, or reliability of something, especially before it is taken into widespread use.* Read that? That means that a woman wants to *establish* (determine, ascertain, etc.) your *quality* as a man, how you will *perform* in certain situations in the future, and whether or not she can *rely* on (trust) you. And she does all of this covertly, unexpectedly, and under the radar of men so that they won't have a chance to lie to her.

Let's look at it this way. If a woman meets a man and asks him, *"So, how much money do you make?"* he can lie. If she asks him, *"Are you an exceptional lover?"* he can lie. If she asks him, *"Will you treat me with respect and be a good father to our children?"* he can lie.

If a college professor wants to know if you've learned everything you needed to know about a certain subject at the end of the semester, she can either ask you if you've learned what you were suppose to or, to avoid the risk of you lying to her she can test you on that subject instead.

Even with this college example, life is a bit unfair because unlike a college exam you have no idea when and sometimes how a woman is going to test you. In the game of love a woman's tests are more like pop quizzes than an end-of-term examination.

Women intrinsically understand that a man can and often WILL lie in order to get with a woman. So during the initial phases of getting to know you, a woman will test you in order to quickly learn a great deal about you without the risk of being misled.

Additionally, an especially attractive woman doesn't have time to deal with all of the guys who may be interested in her. Because of this, she may subconsciously create a flawless system for weeding out unsuitable men who just don't "get it." And once she finds a man who "gets it" she's going to continue to test him until the relationship ends or he kicks the bucket.

On the other hand, when a woman is already in a relationship with a man, she understands that her future well-being is directly linked to the quality of the man that she's already committed to. Therefore, once in a relationship the tests will continue so that she can quickly access where she stands with him and what kind of man he is without the risk of lies and misinformation.

She Can't Control What She Craves

When it comes to relating with men, women are biologically designed by their Maker to seek out love and leadership and not necessarily in that order. These desires aren't something that a woman can consciously control; therefore, it's all too common for her desires to get the best of her. In other words, if a woman longs for love and leadership she's going to do whatever she can to get both of those things from a man.

Some men, when first introduced to the concept that women subconsciously test them at every stage of the mating game, are usually shocked and appalled. Some even struggle with discomfort as they start to distrust women on the whole because it seems so diabolical.

Being hardwired to desire a man's strength, a woman will view her significant other as being at least partially responsible for her well-being. This means that in certain situations, she expects her man to protect her even from herself. The problem here is that these days, most men don't appear to be hardwired this way at all.

Due to cultural shifts, societal issues, and misinformation, men do not assume this responsibility naturally. So when they hear women making statements like *"I need a man who can handle me"* or *"I just wish he'd stand up to me sometimes"* they appear baffled. What's worse is that when women come across these baffled fellows who just don't "get it" they cannot feel nor maintain attraction or respect for them.

Weak, Wavering, and Predatory Men

Weak men are disastrous, wavering men are deceitful, and predatory men are dangerous. A woman will subconsciously test a man she doesn't know to ensure that she won't end up with such a creature.

On the other hand, a woman in a relationship will also test the man she's with if she begins to feel threatened that he's turning into one of these men. If you consider the ramifications for a woman that has devoted her life to one of these types of men you'd have far more sympathy and understanding for her necessity to test.

A weak man has weak principles, weak morals, and no backbone. If she tests him properly, she'll realize that he cannot stand up to her and therefore won't be able to stand up for her. If a man cannot stand up for himself he won't be able to do so for others. He'll have a hell of a time getting what he wants and needs in life because he refuses to assert himself.

A woman simply cannot trust a man like this. Because weak men have difficulty getting their own needs met they won't be able to meet the needs of those dependent on them. Therefore, getting into a relationship with such a creature would put not only her life in jeopardy, but also that of her future offspring. High-quality women learn very quickly that the path to future relationship bliss is highly dependent on a man's ability to stand up for himself.

A wavering man is one who does not know what he wants. He is unsure of himself and unsure of her and often finds himself paralyzed by his indecision and indifference. A woman will test a man to see how much interest he has in her because she instinctively knows that loving her requires a man's full devotion. A man who's only half-hearted about loving her will be easy prey for other women.

No woman wants to end up in a loveless relationship. Such a thing is torture for both the man and the woman involved. Testing a man prior to the beginning of a relationship ensures a woman of the man's level of desire and passion. If he proves himself to be steadfast in his desire and persistent in his passion, it makes it easier for her to let down her guard and give her heart and more to him.

Even during a relationship, she will continue to test him to ensure that his resolve to "love her passionately" has not dissipated over time. She may even test him to stir up the sexual tension that first existed in the beginning of the relationship (something that I discuss later on in the book).

Predatory men pose the greatest threat because unlike the first two types of interested men, these men *consciously* seek to seduce women with malevolent motives. If she is sound of mind a woman will avoid a predatory man at all costs. She wants no dealing with a man whose only intentions for her are vile or completely self-serving in nature. The men I refer to are the abusers (physical and emotional), players, cads, rapists, and even potential murderers.

A woman who finds herself being courted by a predatory man has a lot to lose if his seduction is successful. A relationship with such a man may end in humiliation, loss of reputation, abuse, rape, and even death.

Although I dislike being so grim and dark, we do live in a world where many women have fallen prey to the unkind and monstrous acts of such men. This is a fate that every woman wants to avoid, hence why testing men for strength and quality of character helps them to put the odds in their favor.

The Games Women Play

A woman may test a man in many different ways to see what she can get away with, what kind of man he is, and how invested he is in her. Whether you've just started dating that super hot coworker or you've been married to a wonderful woman for twenty plus years, some if not all of the following situations may seem familiar to you.

Here are a few examples of how you might be tested:

- When your girlfriend blatantly flirts with other men in your presence.

- When your wife seems to feign sexual disinterest to make you work for it.

- When a woman playfully teases you and gives you a hard time.

- When you say or do something she doesn't like and she storms off expecting you to chase her.

- When she cancels a date or changes plans on you at the last minute without a clear apology or explanation.

- When she expects you to know "what's wrong" when she's upset and she gets even more upset when you fail to use your mutant powers of telepathy to figure her out.

- When a woman who's <u>clearly</u> shown romantic interest in you fails to return your phone calls.

- When she asks loaded, no-win questions like, "Is she more attractive than me?" or "Do I look fat to you?"

- When she pressures you to make a cosmetic or style change because she prefers it. (She nit picks about your grooming and choice of clothes.)

- When she gives you "do this or I'll leave you" ultimatums in order to get her way.

- When she demands that you complete chores that have already been determined as her responsibility.

- When she insists on putting you in situations that make you extremely uncomfortable.

- When she blames you for her negative feelings, even though you did absolutely nothing to affect her mood.

- When she pouts, whines, complains, or criticizes

you when you do something that she doesn't approve of.

- When she insults or belittles you in social settings.

- When she responds angrily after you disapprove of something she said or did.

- When she habitually nags you to do things her way.

- When she constantly second-guesses your every decision.

- When she acts like a manipulative, spoiled child just to see how much you'll let her get away with.

- When she requests you to "prove" your love to her when she's "feeling" unloved and undesirable.

- When she expects you to ask for her permission before you do something you want to do or engage in an activity you want to engage in.

- When you try too hard to make her happy and she shows you nothing but contempt and ingratitude.

I could go on but I think you have the picture. A woman can test you anytime and anywhere and in many different ways. It's good to develop a sort of built-in radar for this kind of thing so that you'll know a test when it's happening.

Knowing is half the battle. And in most cases, getting angry or giving in when a woman tests you results in automatic failure. Consistently responding like a mature, masculine man who's in control is the other half of the challenge.

Why You Don't Want to Fail These Tests

As guys become privy to being tested by a woman they may adopt the mindset that "it's not their problem." They think that it shouldn't matter if they fail a woman's tests or not. Who cares if they say or do the wrong thing? If you're a man in control of your own mind and you don't care what she thinks of you, it shouldn't matter if she thinks you failed her "test." Right?

Well, I've got news for you. For the most part, because these tests are done subconsciously she doesn't decide logically whether or not you've passed her test. The entire process happens automatically, which means what *you* think of her test is inconsequential.

A woman can't *help* but feel a sense of loss when you fail, especially if she's romantically interested or emotionally invested in you. Failure, my friend, is not an option if you want the love, respect, support, and sexual interest of a good woman. She cannot help how she's wired, and she's wired to test men in order to survive.

Repeatedly failing a woman's congruence tests results in her losing respect for you; this inevitably causes a loss in her attraction to you. Ultimately, as a woman's respect for and attraction to a man diminishes so does her sexual interest in him. I can think of few things worse than being married to a woman who has zero sexual interest in you.

On the other hand, repeated failure to pass a woman's tests for commitment results in a loss of relationship security on her part. This causes an overall loss of intimacy because she doesn't feel important enough to her man. When her security is threatened a woman will ultimately withdraw her emotions from the relationship leading, again, to loss of physical intimacy and eventually her escape (break-up, divorce, etc.).

As you can see, no matter what you may think about these "tests" that women use on men it's still vitally important to overcome them. That is of course, IF you desire a passionate, harmonious relationship with a woman.

CHAPTER 3:

How Women Test Men

What is a Congruence Test?

A congruence test is any kind of conscious or subconscious behavior a woman exhibits while interacting with a man in order to discover if his external representation is consistent with his inner frame. In simpler terms, it's a test to determine whether or not a man is, at his core, congruent with what he's presenting to her.

Such tests can be non-verbal, such as a woman storming out after an argument while expecting her man to chase after her, thus testing his resolve. These tests can also be verbal and arise in the form of light-hearted teasing, sexual innuendo, backhanded compliments, or even outright insults aimed test to a man's mettle and tolerance.

Men low in confidence or who lack strong personal boundaries, self-belief, and principles struggle the most with congruence tests. This is simply due to the fact that they are, at their core, incongruent from who they pretend to be. While learning effective communication strategies can help a man to overcome these tests, they are at best to be treated as training wheels. The most effective solution for a man is to become more congruent with his actions. This is the path of masculine maturity.

Another side of the congruence test coin is the compliance test. Women use these tests to figure out how compliant a man is with her needs and wants as opposed to his own. These can come in the form of small or large requests that are manipulative in nature in order to test a man's boundaries. In her mind she's trying to assess, *"How much is he willing to please me?"* or *"How much can I get away with before he tells me "NO"?"* These tests can also come in the form of ultimatums as well.

Men who desire a woman's approval above all else struggle the most with compliance type tests. Such men display neediness that women do not find attractive. Whether it's a first encounter or a marriage of twenty plus years, a woman will use compliance tests to get her way or to coerce a man into asserting his boundaries with her. The paradox is, by not complying with such requests or by demanding an equal exchange they end up displaying high self worth.

Some Wives Enjoy Poking the Bear

If you're a married guy, your wife may unknowingly test you if you're mostly a passive, laid back, nice guy and she's learned that she can instigate a more fulfilling sexual experience with you by irritating you. A married man may have unknowingly trained his wife to give him a hard time just so she can get what she wants from him – passionate, wild, uninhibited sex.

Have you ever heard people rave about the magic of make-up sex? That's because when our emotions are intensified it manifests itself through our sexual experiences. It's like being charged up and overwhelmed with emotional intensity, a kind of intensity that will find its outlet in the bedroom. The interesting thing is that it doesn't matter whether these emotions are negative or positive. The intense emotions you feel after your wife tests you (in this case, anger, aggravation, etc.) will explode exactly where she wants it – between her legs.

You may have engineered this sort of reward-based negative behavior in your wife over the years of your marriage if she's figured out that rubbing you the wrong way is going to get her sexually ravished and manhandled in the bedroom. And you may even be surprised to find out just how much your wife actually enjoys being sexually ravished by you when you turn into an insatiable, aggravated mad man. It's like she's trying to poke the docile, lazy bear at the zoo. She WANTS to see it get riled up.

So what if you recognize this kind of behavior in your wife and you'd rather not deal with her tests (but still want the phenomenal sex)? Simple. Learn to recognize when she's being a "bad girl" and just give her what she wants. You can even preemptively turn things up a notch in the bedroom to avoid or at least lessen her attempts to aggravate you.

Every man's wife is going to act differently when she's asking for a good bedroom bullying, so your job is to figure out the cues your wife may be giving you. The faster you figure out that she's unconsciously playing her "piss-him-off-to-get-manhandled" game with you, the easier it will be to circumvent her tests completely and go straight to the phenomenal sex.

Learn how to tap into your most primal masculinity as well as your intense love for her and give her what she's asking for. Supply her with the intense sexual experiences she may require now and then if you realize that your wife has been poking your bear all these years. It may take awhile, but by fulfilling her needs preemptively you can help her realize that she doesn't have to poke the bear to get a good show.

She Wants to Get Off on You

Encountering a woman's congruence tests make absolute sense while dating. She's trying to figure out what kind of man you are and what she can expect from you in the future. But when you're already married, a man of reason may wonder why in the world his wife would continue to test him if he's already proved his worth. Wouldn't it make more sense to just not be tested and enjoy a more peaceful existence with the woman you love? For us guys, it would, but for women…not so much.

The best way to explain this is to think about a woman's need for dramatic interaction between her and her man. Whereas a man is driven by his primal (physical) senses of sight, touch, etc., a woman's sexual driving force is her mind (psychological). Women are stimulated best by sexual tension, the friction of masculine against feminine. In order for her to get that little jolt of sexual excitement from you, she requires a playful assertion of your masculine confidence and power.

So while looking at your wife naked and groping her tight little body gives you the sexual jolt you need, experiencing a first-hand display of your assertiveness gives her what she needs. And the best way for her to accomplish this is to "poke the bear" until she gets a rise out of you.

Would you stop squeezing your wife's breasts once you've already determined that they're firm and fabulous? Of course you wouldn't. Would you stop groping her butt when she least expects it even though you already know the goods are still top quality? No, because at this point in the game you're no longer assessing her quality, you're *enjoying* her.

In the same way, just because your wife has tested you in the past doesn't mean it's going to stop now. Yes, she's already assessed your quality but sometimes she just wants to *enjoy* you. For her, poking the bear is highly enjoyable. It's a way for her to experience your masculinity.

For some men, being objectified this way may be disturbing because they have no control over it. But just how your wife may not always enjoy being groped at random hours of the day, you're not going to enjoy every single one of her random attempts to rile you up.

In any event, don't worry about it. If she's testing you she desires you. So instead of waiting for her to start poking just give her a show. Preemptive need meeting in this area will decrease her need to test you.

Deciphering a Woman's Test in a Request

If a woman storms off after an argument and she's expecting you to chase behind her, you can be sure it's a test. If she playfully teases you to evoke a sexual response from you (poking the bear) you know she's testing you.

While these types of tests are easy to figure out, other types of female testing may not be so obvious. This is especially the case if the test comes in the form of a request. And it can get really confusing, especially if you never realized that you were being tested on a regular basis.

You could always solve this by thinking that any request she makes of you is a test, but that sort of thinking isn't conducive to maintaining a happy and harmonious *adult* relationship. Living in fear of being manipulated will make you paranoid. It keeps you on the defensive and makes it ridiculously difficult for you to enjoy a loving relationship with any woman. So instead of thinking that every time she asks you to do something she's testing you, it's better to cue in on your woman's *tone* and the underlying *motive* she has when she makes a request.

The best solution I've come across for telling whether or not a request is a test based on a woman's tone and motive comes from the relationship author, Athol Kay. On his blog, MarriedManSexLife.com, [1] Athol posits that a woman's request can be placed in one of four categories.

First, he mentions that a reasonable request made in a reasonable tone is not a test and therefore should not be treated like one. If your wife or girlfriend makes a sensible request of you in a very graceful tone, she's just looking for a little assistance. For example, *"Honey, can you get the flour for me please. It's in the top cupboard."* You're clearly taller than her and she's baking your favorite cookies. Comply with it.

I always encourage guys to reward good behavior with good behavior. If your woman makes a reasonable request of you in a reasonable tone, the last thing you want to do is respond harshly. Don't give her any incentive to treat you like an inconsiderate brute.

The second type of request Athol discusses is a reasonable request made in an unreasonable tone. These can be classified as true congruence tests because of the way a woman approaches you. Her request is sincere and necessary but her tone is disrespectful. For example, *"Honey, get off your lazy behind and get me the flour NOW."* Do not comply with nagging or any kind of cantankerous behavior. Firmly tell her that you'll address her needs when she changes her tone to a more reasonable one.

Thirdly, Athol discusses unreasonable requests made in a reasonable tone. These are, in fact, compliance tests. You'll recognize them because whatever she's asking for seems so unreasonable, but she asks in a very pleasant, attractive tone just to appease your ego. It's usually something that would cost you so much of your time, money, standards, etc., that it makes you undeniably uncomfortable.

For example, *"Honey, I was thinking we should buy a better car. The business is doing really well, and we can afford it. What do you think?"* A smart woman might even apply some logic to her request, but when you observe the underlying motive you'll realize what's going on. The truth is you don't *need* a second car and even though you *can* afford it, it's still not a part of your financial plans for the year.

How do you handle it? You can discuss it like an adult and help her realize that you really don't need a second car right now. You can even take it a step further and give a cocky response complete with a sly grin, *"Well, keep thinking about it."* Whatever you do though, do not comply. She's being downright manipulative, whether she realizes it or not.

The fourth category Athol mentions is an unreasonable request made in an unreasonable tone. This is blatant verbal abuse, boundary crossing, and disrespectful language that must be dealt with firmly. For example, *"John, why are you such a cheapskate? I hate being seen driving that piece of crap in our garage. I want a new car, John. You're so selfish when it comes to money."*

If she's acting like this you can either ignore her entirely or firmly tell her that you refuse to even communicate with her until she changes her tone. If she continues her tirade and you feel your anger slowly peak, remove yourself from her presence before you do or say something you might regret.

In this instance, the woman is being both manipulative and mean. Do not comply and if possible, do not even communicate. You are neither a child nor an animal. You're a man and you expect to be treated like one.

As a final note, Athol mentions that certain requests may actually be mission critical in that they require your immediate attention. It doesn't matter if it's a test or not because certain things just need to get done as soon as possible. These include home maintenance, paying bills, and usually emergencies related to family. As the man of the house there will be times when you'll have to bite the bullet and comply not because you're caving to her pressure, but because of your commitment to the greater good.

The great thing about this whole approach is that it's especially useful when you're in doubt as to whether or not you should comply, put your foot down and say *"NO"*, or simply ignore her until she changes her tone.

In his best-selling book, *Married Man Sex Life Primer: 2011*, Athol calls these tests "Fitness Tests" and discusses the various types and how a married man can overcome them. It's a noteworthy read for all married men, but especially if you're a husband looking for a permanent solution for getting your wife more interested in having sex with you (and only you). Highly recommended.

Reference: [1] Kay, Athol. "Fitness Testing: Fail To Comply With The Request." Web blog post. *MarriedManSexLife*. September 28 2011. Web. December 2013.

Understanding Commitment Tests

There's another type of test that guys in relationships may experience more often than not. These are the kinds of tests women use to gain some assurance on the level of a man's commitment to them.

Interestingly enough, commitment tests usually only show up when a woman begins to feel that your loyalty to her is threatened. If she begins to feel as if your priorities are elsewhere, that you've lost interest in her, or that she can be easily replaced at the drop of a dime she's going to start throwing commitment tests at you in order to ease her insecurities.

If you haven't realized already, commitment tests are normally a problem when a man is acting so overwhelmingly dominant with a woman that he fails to balance his displays of firm leadership with displays of unconditional love. Whereas congruence tests of various kinds must be overcome with overt to subtle displays of masculine assertiveness, commitment tests must be overcome with overt to subtle displays of emotional interest.

Acting indifferent, stubborn, or even amused when a woman is begging to see if you really do care about her will only make things worse. Her insecurity will skyrocket as she starts displaying increased behaviors of sexual disinterest, doubt, disrespect, anxiety, and discomfort in your presence. This sort of behavior is actually a defense mechanism. She acts this way for one of two reasons:

1. She's preparing herself for your eventual departure or...

2. She's emotionally distancing herself from you to initiate her own preemptive exit from the relationship.

If you're always assertive, strong-willed, firm, and uncompromising, over time your woman might begin to feel as if she won't be able to keep you. In order for a woman to feel a deep sense of emotional comfort in a relationship she must be constantly reassured of a man's emotional investment.

Being dominant to the point where you fail to show a woman tenderness, kindness, compassion, and empathy will make her believe that one day you might just up and leave her for a younger/newer model if she fails to meet your standards. In other words, a woman needs to feel as if she has some sort of emotional foothold on you, an anchor if you will, that'll always keep you bonded to her. She doesn't want to *feel* easily replaceable.

Because she wants to know that she has at least some influence in your life her commitment tests can only be overcome by displays of emotion or demonstrations of love and desire. But unfortunately, to the untrained eye a commitment test may seem like a congruence test if you're not fully attuned to a woman's needs. Again, things like disrespect, neediness, tit-for-tat behavior, emotional meltdowns, angry outbursts, whining, and pining are signs that a need is not being met.

The Tough but Tender Approach

Although the problem might have stemmed from being too controlling or too alpha male, in overcoming a woman's commitment test you must maintain a frame of leadership. If you act like a supplicating wussy even when she's emotional every time she tests you in this way, you're actually training her to use her tears, fears, etc., to elicit a favorable emotional response from you.

A man should always maintain his boundaries but be willing to open up those boundaries to win-win solutions. When a woman desires reassurance of your commitment to her, the best and first thing to do is to approach her like an adult and openly *communicate* the issue at hand.

The reason she's acting out is because she feels taken for granted, unimportant to you, or replaceable. When she's feeling unloved you may need to learn how to pick up the changes in her behavior much quicker in order to take the initiative in getting her to communicate her needs in a respectful, healthy way.

Once again, as the man you must take the lead, even if her emotions are absolutely frightening. You must encourage her to communicate her needs like an adult by taking charge and giving her your undivided attention while showing her empathy.

Assuming she's been using passive-aggressive behaviors (like the silent treatment) to get your attention, you must push through these feints and get to the heart of the matter. The best communication technique for getting through to the heart of a matter is called Active Listening.

The late Stephen Covey, in his phenomenal book, *The 7 Habits of Highly Effective People*, discusses this communication technique in great depth. It's a communication technique used in counseling and conflict resolution that requires the listener to confirm what the speaker is saying by re-stating or paraphrasing what they hear. This helps the speaker to feel a sense of affirmation from the listener, which compels them to open up even more, thus eventually getting to the heart of the matter. For example:

John: "You've been giving me the silent treatment all morning. I love you, but I'm only going to ask you once. Why are you acting this way?"

Beth: "You haven't made an effort to do anything special with me ever since you got that promotion. I'm beginning to think that job is more important to you than me and the kids."

John: "So you're saying that you feel as if I've been neglecting you lately."

Beth: "Yes, I do. I don't like it when you come home late everyday. My dad used to do it and it drove my mother crazy."

John: "You feel as if your dad's workaholism ruined your parent's marriage."

Beth: "Yes. I don't want us to end up like my parents, John. I really don't."

John: "I promise you, Beth. We won't end up like your parents. Here's what I'll do…"

I know, I know. I should write screenplays for a living. But as my dramatic, heart-warming example shows, active listening is a great way to get to the heart of the matter in order to solve conflicts.

Notice that John starts the conversation both firm and tender. With steady resolve he acknowledges the change in her behavior and is determined to work through it, as long as she's willing to communicate like an adult. By leading the conversation this way he maintains his frame of leadership while showing her that he cares about her.

The key to maintaining a leadership frame even in the midst of a commitment test that demands your tenderness is to encourage her to communicate *like an adult*. Don't chase her mood swings or supplicate her even when she's needy. If you do you're enabling her to act out whenever she feels insecure. This will make you a slave to her emotions, and she might be tempted to exploit this weakness in the future.

The best thing to do is to show a low tolerance for passive-aggressive behaviors like the silent treatment. If you tell her *"I'll only ask you once"* and she refuses to speak…stay true to your word. Treat her like an adult and expect her to act like one. You should expect her to hold you to that same standard as well.

Once you've taken the time to *really* listen to her, sympathize with her, and connect with her needs, take it a step further and meet whatever need she requires in order to gain assurance of your love and commitment. She may need an act of romantic expression, a warm, passionate embrace, or even something as simple as the words, *"I'll never stop loving you"* to make her feel secure again.

If what she really needs from you is an act of sacrifice, just like the example above, approach it from a win-win position. John may not be able to come home early every single day, but he can try to reach an agreement with his wife that he'll make an effort to be home earlier at least three or four days out of five.

Compromise doesn't have to be an ugly word in which men think they're giving up what they want. It's all about finding win-win solutions and even knowing when to make a sacrifice for the greater good. Consider it a blessing when a good woman craves your love and loyalty. As you become the stronger, more assertive man whom she can respect, desire, and support, don't let her doubt your commitment.

I must close out this section with a warning. Only you can know your woman. Sometimes if she *feels* that you don't show your love enough and she *demands* something from you, she might be being manipulative. If she *demands* that you romance her, take her out more, buy her things, etc., or else…she's actually trying to guilt you into meeting her *demands*.

There's a difference between a woman who has *needs* that must be met for her to feel secure in the relationship and a woman who has *wants* that she demands you to fulfill just to appease her. This is why learning your woman's behaviors and <u>actively listening</u> to her is vital. Only through clear communication will you understand the difference and avoid becoming her emotional slave.

CHAPTER 4:
Communicating with a Testing Woman

In Control but Not Controlling

Women want men who are in control of themselves but not controlling of others. In the face of conflict and confrontation a woman wants a man to rise to the occasion and respond with calmness, confidence, and calculated decision-making. If you're terrified of confrontation and your idea of being 'in control' is by *forcing* your will and desires on others, you're not a man of who's in control.

Being a man 'in control' means that you are able to display *grace under pressure* while in the midst of difficult situations. A woman may test you to find out whether or not you're a man who's capable of handling confrontations and challenges with tact, poise, and even a sense of humor. She wants to know if you can rationally handle her irrational emotions, stand up to her, or "vibe" with her on an emotionally-charged level. And in order to display this grace under pressure it is imperative for a man to maintain his *frame*.

Your frame is the method of interpretation you use to comprehend a certain event or situation. In simpler terms, your frame is a set of self-beliefs that determine how you define the outside world in relation to yourself. Keep in mind that the most important factor in how you respond depends on the frame you choose as you interact with a woman.

For example, responding from a frame in which you see yourself as a "prized catch", a man of strength, authority, and leadership, will communicate confidence and therefore the congruence she's testing you for. Responding from a frame of "unworthiness" in which you place yourself in a position of submission, supplication, and approval seeking, communicates your uncertainty. If you're in a relationship, her tests will continue to escalate until you get it right. If you're just getting to know her she might just lose complete interest in you altogether.

If You're Selling It You'd Better Believe in It

The whole point of testing a man for congruence is to see if he believes his own press. A woman wants to know if what a man is presenting is in fact, the real deal. In other words, if you really don't believe in what you're selling, she'll know soon enough.

For example, if you're extremely confident in a particular area in your life it may come off as arrogant to *some* people. As this confident display piques a woman's interest she may manifest her curiosity with a question like, *"Are you always this arrogant?"*

Now, a man less convinced of his own righteousness might begin to question himself. Such a man will respond in an approval seeking way by saying, *"Well, not really. I'm just kidding you know?"* or in a nervous manner to hide his shame, *"You've got me all wrong. I'm not that kind of guy. I'm actually a really modest guy!"*

Again, fail.

In this example, the woman has succeeded in finding the truth about him as she thinks, *"Oh! So he IS arrogant and is trying to convince me otherwise in order to gain my approval or he's acting arrogant because he really isn't that confident in himself after all."*

Either way, this self-doubting response is a sign that

this man has placed a higher value on this woman's opinion about him than on his own opinion. He has unknowingly surrendered his own self-perceptions in favor of one he *thinks* she might approve of and thusly FAILS her test.

At the opposite end of the scale is the man who thinks that anyone who has an opinion divergent from his own is an idiot that must be punished. Such men usually respond with spitefulness or aggression if they feel they are being challenged. Whereas the first guy responded like a supplicating wussy, this guy might respond in a more irritated tone and say something like, *"Are you always this annoying?"*

Granted, such a comeback may work on *some* women, particularly those who enjoy verbal sparring with the opposite sex. But depending on the rapport between the two in this example, it won't have the desired effect.

This interaction could be even worse if this guy takes her test as a personal affront and starts calling her names. This is obviously something a classy gentleman such as yourself won't want to do. There are better ways to deal with a woman who's testing your congruence without being a wussy or trying to control the situation.

The man whose disposition rests at the sweet equilibrium between passivity and aggression knows what it means to be assertive and has full control of himself. In this example, he is a man fully convinced of his own righteousness and will see her question for what it is – *her* opinion.

To her, whether he's being arrogant or not is inconsequential. The purpose of her questioning was really to find out whether or not his outward actions are a product of supreme inner confidence or camouflaged insecurities.

So what might be a better response? Well, that depends on his certainty (or what's congruent with his reality). If he really does come across as arrogant sometimes, then he shouldn't try to hide it. Like this:

Her: "Are you always this arrogant?"

Him (with an overconfident grin): "So I've been told."

This is a simple, firm, and honest response that succinctly says, *"I don't care what you think of me."* No games or gimmicks, and if she's a woman of quality she'll immediately get the message that he actually does believe his own press and he's comfortable in his own skin. In short, this is a man who's in control of himself.

Keep in mind that I'm not condoning men to behave like arrogant, inconsiderate brutes. The main idea to gather from this section is to not allow other's opinions of you to determine whether or not you *approve* of yourself.

We all have room for improvement in terms of character development, and even an arrogant man can show his humility by how he handles his detractors. In fact, being honest with others about your flaws is a major key to building relationships. I discuss how to do this effectively in another chapter.

Calling Out Her Negative Behaviors

Have enough guts to call your woman out on her negative or unattractive behaviors. I'm not talking about giving her a hard time if she makes an honest mistake and she's sincerely apologetic for it. I'm talking about putting a spotlight on a woman's consistent negative behaviors; things like disrespectfulness, rudeness, manipulation, pettiness, etc.

Anything she does that clearly communicates that she's acting unreasonable, being manipulative, or disrespectful is grounds for being called out. The same applies for her unattractive behavior that clearly communicates low character, i.e. lying, stealing, slander, etc.

I've heard women say that they like being with a man who knows when to call them out on their unattractive behavior. This isn't new knowledge unless you've been raised on a deserted island somewhere so it shouldn't come as a shock to you.

A quality woman doesn't want to be with a man she can walk all over like a doormat. While she may enjoy the pleasing, supplicating nature of such a man for a short period of time, she'll quickly realize how irritating and unmanly (unattractive) he actually is. In short, men who always give women what they want and who *let them* get away with bad behavior are repulsive to women.

Imagine you are driving in the car with the woman you love and you both are enjoying playful banter and great conversation. Eventually, she starts talking about a situation at work that upset her and you hear her out to let her vent. You progressively notice however, that she's no longer just talking about a situation but she's actually badmouthing another human being, and she's being really nasty about it.

If this sort of behavior is highly distasteful to you, you might grow irritated. If you know your wife or girlfriend is "better than that" based on her overall character, listening to her badmouth another person turns you off. So what do you do when such behavior is making you uncomfortable? You call it out…like a man.

Here's an example as to how this might play out:

Her: "That's why I can't stand Maria. She's a bimbo and a _____, and I hate having to put up with her stupid _____ around the office. Everything about her makes me sick. Even her husband is a complete piece of…."

Him: "Okay, that's enough. Look, I don't mind you venting to me but I'm not going to listen to you if you insist on defaming this person. It's very unattractive and I know you're better than this."

Her: "Are you serious?"

Him: "Yes. Save this sort of thing for your girlfriends. I'll have no part of it."

In this example all you're doing is setting a boundary. You're not trying to control or change her, you're just making it clear that you won't endorse this kind of behavior and that you'd prefer it if she cease and desist. Of course, you may receive a snippy comment after you've spoken your mind but it's best to just ignore it. Give her time to process what you just said.

If you're consistent about it you'll come to realize that a high-quality woman will actually admire when you're honest with her about her behavior. It tells her that you truly care about the quality of her character and expect high standards for her. Women, just like men, need a bit of tough love every now and then too.

Of course, if you decided to be the "Nice Guy" instead and just let it slide…again, she'll continue on in her unattractive behavior until it completely turns you off and frustrates you. The result? You become passive-aggressive and avoid her because of how "annoying" she is. Had you pointed out the annoying behavior in the first place you wouldn't have to endure it. A man should not complain against that which he allows to torment him.

The key to successfully influencing a woman when you call out her negative behavior is consistency. If you're inconsistent she's not going to believe you're for real. If you're The Big Bad Wolf while on vacation with your family but back home you're Mr. Nice Guy, she's not going to take you seriously, and neither will anyone else for that matter.

Don't think that you can be two different people around her just because the environment or situation changes. Your frame must be consistent if you want to be taken seriously.

If you still feel at a complete loss when it comes to communicating your needs or even criticizing another person, check out the best-selling book by Dale Carnegie called, _How to Win Friends and Influence People_. If you haven't heard of it, it's a communications book that'll show you how to speak your mind with confidence without ruining your relationships. Sometimes it IS what you say AND how you say it that counts. It's an excellent book if you want to improve your ability to reprove a woman respectfully so that you don't break any emotional glass.

A Word of Caution

It is exceedingly difficult to get a woman to *accept* your disapproval of her behavior and change to please you if she isn't already highly attracted to you or emotionally invested in you. I say this mainly to two groups of guys:

1. Single guys who find themselves compelled to reproach a woman they barely know and...

2. Guys in relationships with women who have little to no respect for them.

As I've already discussed, the guys in the latter group have a problem with consistency. As for the guys in the former, the problem isn't consistency; it's a matter of *authorization*.

If you have just begun dating a woman and her interest in you hasn't developed to the point where she's completely infatuated with you, attempts to curb her negative behavior might end the courtship. Why?

Her investment in you is so miniscule that she won't feel compelled to submit to your brand of masculine *authority*. She'll probably think to herself that it's in her best interest to move on and find a man "less demanding" (more accepting of her bad behavior) than stick around to put up with such a "control freak" (man with boundaries).

In the early stages of dating, a man and woman will always try to put their best foot forward in order to maintain the illusion of being the ideal catch. Some women may play aloof, some won't play games at all, but few will easily yield to the desires of a man they have not yet approved of as "worthy" to lead them. To make matters even more difficult, the things she finds attractive about you can be rationalized away in her mind rather swiftly if she feels as if you have no right to reprove her.

Of course, whether she might respond favorably or not shouldn't determine how you deal with negative behavior. It's much better to be clear about what you want as early on as possible. The good part about this is if you do call her out on her negative behavior and she apologizes, she's probably worth keeping around.

The other benefit here is that you can actually gauge a woman's capacity to accept a man's leadership by the way she responds to your sincere disapproval. If she consciously works at curbing her behavior to please you, it's a sign that she respects your boundaries. In this case, you've got a winner on your hands.

On the flip side, if she rejects what you have to say no matter how rational you are, chances are she'll be too much trouble to deal with later on anyway. As with all things, being honest and clear with your boundaries will help you separate the chaff from the wheat when it comes to finding a quality woman.

I'll admit that such situations are quite delicate and require tact, confidence, and a sort of amused mastery when it comes to dealing with women. You may have just met what appears to be a great girl and as you are getting to know her you realize that she has ways about her that you find disrespectful.

At the end of the day, it's up to you to decide how to proceed forward. If you're more interested in game playing, you might make more allowances for her behavior. But if you're a man who truly appreciates the candor and kindness of high-character women, you are likely to show less forbearance for undesirable behavior.

Reframing Your Displeasure for Her Pleasure

If you want to communicate your displeasure or dissatisfaction to your woman without coming off like a complete jerk try reframing the situation for both of your benefits. It all comes down to communication. And as I've probably repeated a thousand times already, *sometimes* it's not what you say but how you say it that matters most in a relationship.

For example, let's say that on your path to being radically honest with the woman you love, you feel the urge to tell her just how much you despise a pair of shoes that she seems to wear all the time. It's not that she wears them for beauty; she loves them because they're comfortable. And every single time she puts them on you want to tell her just how ugly they are and how unattractive they make her look overall. But you never speak your mind because you're too afraid of hurting her feelings or inviting her fury. So what's a man to do? Simple. Reframe your displeasure for her pleasure.

So instead of telling her just how ugly the shoes are you can reframe the situation by telling her that her shoes don't match up to her beauty. Reframe your displeasure to communicate to her that you think the shoes are below her standards and that you'd like for her to purchase a new pair, one that's more comfortable and attractive.

Tell her this in a confident but laid-back tone. You're not commanding her to change her shoes; you're simply expressing your disapproval in a sincere way. This shows her that you actually pay special interest to her appearance and that *you* enjoy seeing her at her best.

Notice that I said "you" enjoy seeing her at her best. If you honestly believe that she gains pleasure by being visually pleasing she'll believe it as well. But you have to communicate your displeasure in a confident and at times, playful tone in order to boost her self-esteem while making her mindful of what you want.

Ignore the Bait

Sometimes, no wait…A LOT of times; your woman is going to tempt you to take the bait. She's going to say something designed to get a certain emotional response from you and it's going to come when you *least* expect it. I guarantee you, that if you take the bait…you're in for a hell of a ride. Heck, if you even *acknowledge* that the bait exists, you're already too far down the rabbit hole.

Anytime you find yourself responding with a "What exactly is that suppose to mean?" in an annoyed or hurt tone of voice, you can just stamp FAIL on your forehead and call it a day. When situations like this arise, the best thing you can do for both you and your woman is to *ignore the bait*.

Let's say you just initiated a discussion about something that interests you. It's a harmless conversation and you never had any intention of it leading into her getting upset, slighted, or offended. But she does. Something you say changes her mood, fast. You see it all over her face, you hear it in her voice, and you notice that her statements become more and more edgy, almost as if she's *looking* for a fight (one that you won't win).

What's actually happening is that you're being baited, slowly but surely, into a discussion that you never had any intention of getting into. For some reason, something you said taps into an insecurity she has and how you respond to her prodding, edgy statements will make all the difference in whether you're able to secure a win or a loss.

How do you know when her insecurities are flaring up and you're being baited into a hornet's nest? Easy. The moment she says something that causes every single red alarm to sound off inside your head, you're being baited. The moment she says something that makes your heart skip a beat because you just know where this is headed, you're being baited. It will differ from situation to situation, but you WILL know. You might even get a sick feeling in your stomach as past arguments flashback in your mind in mere moments.

Regardless of how her baiting affects you, it will trigger something in you that will warn you of impending danger. This is the point of no return, and crossing this point with her usually doesn't end well for either of you. So what do you do when you reach this ill-fated communicative threshold? Simple. You *ignore the bait*.

Because the thing she said to you will trigger an emotional reaction within you, you have a few fleeting moments to *choose* how you respond to her. Keep in mind however, that in this scenario the snarky statement she makes will not be posed as a question. You cannot ignore a question. So if she asks you a question ignoring the bait won't work. But more often than not, her remark will be an attempt to "get the last word", in order to tick you off, coerce you to apologize, or run after her.

She's insecure and she (perhaps subconsciously) wants you to know about it. And the best way she's going to accomplish this is to say something that, based on her experience with you, she *knows* is going to trigger a negative emotional response from you that's favorable to her. And consider this: sometimes a woman will do this in an effort to curb your future behavior. She might actually want you to have a negative association with the topic at hand so that you'll avoid doing whatever you did to evoke her insecurities in the future. Pure genius.

I'm one-hundred percent positive that in these situations a man can totally ignore the bait and pass this test with flying colors. Why? Because I eventually learned that when a woman is insecure about something you said she will say certain things to escalate a normal conversation into a communication nightmare that's designed to make you lose your cool or chase after her.

Every time one of these tests was lobbed at me it was done so to make me feel guilt, shame, anger, or a nauseating concoction of all three. If I felt guilty enough, I'd chase her to apologize. If I felt shame, I'd chase her to make her feel happy again. And if I felt anger, well, we'd get into a senseless argument that usually led to nowhere fast.

Don't get me wrong, I have no problems apologizing when I know that I'm wrong or when I offend my wife. The problem occurs when a man finds himself constantly apologizing for his woman's insecurities. Sometimes it's not *your* problem…it's hers. You're not personally responsible for a woman's insecurities. I mention this because remembering that "it's not about me…it's her" at the very moment she triggers that emotional response is crucial to keeping your composure and ignoring her tantalizing bait.

Realizing that you're not responsible for making her feel happy whenever her emotions get the best of her is powerful. In that moment, you can let her emotions wash over you without *taking it personally*. The moment you take it personally, you take the bait; hook, line, and sinker.

When you keep your composure after a snarky remark that's clearly designed to bait you, you're much more able to see her behavior for what it is – a test – and you're much more capable of walking away from it. In situations like this, choosing not to play her game is a victory in and of itself. By ignoring the bait you can address the issue at another time when she's not feeling as vulnerable.

A woman whose emotions have been compromised due to her insecurities will attempt to shake you as well. When she dangles the bait (her snarky statement) in front of you, ignore it, maintain your composure, and if needed, address it when you both have more emotional balance.

Disarming Her Bombs

Certain kinds of tests women give men are like mini bombs designed to explode on both the unsuspecting or the uninitiated. If you find yourself in the midst of a loaded congruence test in which you know you can't escape, the best thing you can do is disarm it.

An effective communication strategy for disarming her test is to first agree with her then exaggerate her statement in a playful, teasing way. This shows her that you're not afraid of upsetting her, that you've got moxie, that you won't lie to her, and that you're not going to "fall for that" trap again.

By agreeing and exaggerating her statement or question you're using wit to reframe her challenge into something a lot less threatening. Think of it as taking the bite out of her bark or taking the venom out of her sting. You're essentially turning lemons into lemonade by neutralizing her words.

By agreeing you're communicating that you're actually empathizing with her point of view. By exaggerating you're communicating that her statement/question is, in fact, absurd. Simply put, it's a communication strategy for getting her to realize just how irrational/bizarre her statement/question really is.

All this must be done in a confident, self-amused, playful way. You're not insulting her; you're just making light fun of her to highlight the absurdity of what she's saying. Also keep in mind that when a woman is more receptive to your leadership, this technique will work with flying colors.

If she hasn't been thoroughly convinced of your masculine assertiveness, things may get worse before they get better. As I mention elsewhere in this book, consistency is key if you're determined to develop a relationship dynamic where you lead and she supports your leadership.

If you're already in a relationship with a woman or plan to be someday, I suggest you study a few of the following examples to fully grasp how agreeing and exaggerating can disarm her nagging, teasing, or testing statements:

Her: "You actually think you're handsome?"
You: "Of course, you know you can't help yourself around all this man candy."

***

Her: "Are you just going to play video games all day?"
You: "You bet. And with enough practice I can quit my job and do this full-time."

***

Her: "We're watching this movie again?"
You: "It's great isn't it? I'm so glad you're excited!"

***

Her: "Do I look stupid to you?"
You: "I think you look amazing." *wink*

***

Her: "Are you always this late?"
You: "Only when I'm picking up beautiful women."

***

Her: "You never listen to me."
You: "What's that now?"

As always, a word of caution: If these responses turn her into a frisky kitten and she starts to verbally tease you as well, you're winning. If you make her smirk, giggle, or she hits you on the arm in a playful way, you're winning. Even if you get a mild sigh of annoyance and a bratty eye roll, you're still winning.

However, if she continues to flare up in your face and escalate her antagonistic behavior, something deeper may be going on that actually *needs* your attention. If this is the case, you may want to turn the knob down on the playfulness and take her a bit more seriously for the moment. Either that, or as I mentioned before, she hasn't had consistent exposure to your assertiveness and therefore she's not "buying" your act…yet.

Light-hearted teasing, witty repartee, and over the top sarcasm are all effective ways at disarming a woman's congruence test as long as it is, in fact, a test. These examples aren't one-size-fits-all scenarios and the responses won't work if she's actually trying to get more from you than a confirmation of your strength and confidence.

Remember, not everything a woman says or does is a test, but when it is a test, agreeing and exaggerating will be your ace-in-the-hole. This is the key to communicating with her in a way that sparks attraction rather than resentfulness and contempt.

The Three-Word Neutralizer

Another great way to respond to a woman who is clearly communicating with you in a hostile tone is to wait until she's finished her tirade, look her squarely in the eyes, and in a calm, firm, masculine tone, ask her, *"Are you done?"* If she's clearly been communicating in a disrespectful or antagonistic way just to trigger an emotional reaction from you, show her none.

A woman's test may come in the form of hostile displays of emotionally charged behavior that's specifically designed to make you lose your cool. Women sometimes do this consciously just to see if they can easily get to you. A lot of guys unknowingly fall into this trap by losing their cool as they end up in a pointless quarrel or hopeless argument with their woman. By playing her game you fail the test and she loses a little bit more respect for you in the process.

So what's the answer? Simple. Show her that you're not going to play her little game by totally destroying her emotional tirade with a calm, confident response. The sentence, *"Are you done?"* perfectly illustrates exactly what's going on in your head. This short response tells her that you're not going to take part in her game, that you're not impressed with her attempts to shake/break you, and that even though you acknowledge the fact that she needed to "act out" you're ready for her to act like an adult once again.

This statement has the potential to either escalate her hostility or obliterate her aggression altogether. Use the momentary lull to firmly communicate that you'd prefer not to be talked to in such a disrespectful way in the future. If she continues with her aggression, simply walk off and refuse to endure such abuse. If your three-word disarmament calms her down and makes her realize that she's being unreasonable, give her a confident smile and end it with this: *"Nice to have you back."*

Risky? You bet. Rewarding? Absolutely.

CHAPTER 5:

Be Your Own Man and Earn Her Respect

Why You Might Be Afraid of Her

Does your behavior and conversations with your wife or girlfriend resemble a relationship between a strong man and a woman that craves him or does it resemble a relationship between a little boy who's terrified of upsetting his mommy? Think about it.

It's important to be aware of which one it is because any attempt to lead a woman who doesn't respect your authority will end in spectacular failure. She needs to be convinced that *you're convinced* that you're the one wearing the pants in the relationship.

No woman *in her right mind* is going to be attracted to her child. So if you act like a little boy who's afraid of upsetting mommy she will unhappily take on the role you've unknowingly forced on her.

It has probably never even occurred to some guys that their wives or girlfriends continue to test them because they actually want them to push back. A woman would rather feel an intense attraction and adoration for a strong, authoritative man than feel contempt for a fearful, approval-seeking wimp.

By cowering in fear of her emotions you're actually signaling to her that *she* possesses the authority in the relationship and that you'll do just about anything to avoid her wrath, sadness, moodiness, or rejection. If making her emotionally uncomfortable makes you uncomfortable, you're afraid of her.

Sometimes you can tell if a relationship stands a chance based on how much importance a man places on his woman's approval. Women who subconsciously see their husbands and boyfriends as children or little brothers that they have to take care of have a much harder time respecting them.

Over time these women may grow to despise their husbands and boyfriends simply due to the fact that they can no longer *feel* the attraction that once existed. It is extremely difficult for a woman to fall in love and stay in love with a man whom she does not or cannot respect. The best way a man can tell if he wears the pants in his relationship or not is how he interacts with his woman when he knows without a shadow of a doubt that she won't approve of his words or actions. Read that sentence again.

The best example of this concept at work is how ready and willing a man is to lie to his woman just to avoid her "punishment." If you find yourself lying to your wife or girlfriend because you're terrified of upsetting her, you're not being much of a man. If a woman's emotional state determines how honest you are you're not living your life by your principles, you're living it based on her approval.

Here are a few of the most common lies men tell women:

"I'll be there soon."

No, you won't. You're running late and you won't arrive anytime "soon." Tell her the truth. Something like, *"I'm running late."* Short, succinct, and non-avoidant.

"Yes, I did it already." ...Or... "I'm finishing up now."

No, you probably didn't. You forgot, she asked, and now you're *going* to do it. Tell her something like, *"No, I didn't. Thanks for the reminder. I'll get on it after*

_____." It's important that you don't insult a woman's intelligence by using vague terms like "later" or "soon." Give her a definite point in time. Be responsible.

"I didn't know that was today."

You probably did know but you're hoping that your convenient amnesia is going to help you wiggle out of something you don't want to do. If you don't want to do something, tell her you don't want to do something. Don't be a passive little wussy.

"I'm okay. Everything's fine."

No, it isn't. You're in a bad mood and you don't want to discuss it. Either that or she did something to upset you and you don't want to show signs of weakness. It's too late, she probably already knows. You'll be a better man by just being honest about needing some space from her for a while or by telling her exactly how you feel. I've been guilty of this phrase more times than I can count.

"It didn't cost that much."

Poppycock. It probably did but you're afraid that she's going to disapprove of your purchase. If mutual agreement about money expenditure is a priority in your relationship then telling her the truth is always the best option. On the other hand, if how you spend your money is none of her concern you might want to express to her those very sentiments, albeit in a cocky, playful way.

"I didn't have a signal." …Or… "My phone was off." …Or… "I missed your call."

All lies. You were screening her call for whatever reason and you didn't want to answer. If you're having a good time with friends and you fear picking up the phone and telling her that you can't talk right now, you're acting like a child. I can't imagine a mature, masculine man being afraid to let his woman know that he's busy at the moment and will return her call later.

These are just a few simple examples but I'm sure you get the point. As men, we sometimes have the bad habit of telling our women these little white lies just to avoid confrontation and seeming punishment. We're all fond of taking the easy way out because we're creatures of comfort that prefer the path of least resistance. The problem with thinking this way is that we fail to consider the long-term repercussions such behaviors might have in our relationships.

Be a Man About It – Show Some Backbone

Every relationship requires balance. Being dishonest with your woman makes you less of a man; therefore, that masculine feminine balance will always be in question.

A strong, masculine man is assertive, confident, and calm under pressure, regardless if he's at fault or not. He doesn't deviate from his principles to supplicate a woman. He follows through with the truth no matter the consequences and he's willing to suffer pain for the truth. Would such a man lie to his woman just to avoid displeasing her? No.

Living in fear of displeasing a woman turns a man into a dishonest liar, a fraud, and a charlatan. If you believe the key to a "blissful relationship" is through not rocking the boat, you're in for a very rude awakening. Sidestepping her questions, lying, or avoiding conflict won't make her happy, they'll only increase her contempt for you.

So as you interact with your wife or girlfriend, now and again you must ask yourself, *"Am I acting like a man of integrity or am I being conflict-avoidant like a frightened child who thinks he's in trouble?"* Believe me, if you consider the pain of tolerating a sexless marriage, going through divorce, or being in a relationship with a nagging girlfriend, the pain of being a man of integrity who's not afraid to tell his woman the truth is much more bearable.

For the record, I'm not yelling from a soapbox because like most men, I've struggled with this at times throughout my own relationships. Just like anything else becoming a man of integrity requires constant practice and a strong conviction to tell the truth, take responsibility, and suffer the consequences of *your* actions, whatever they may be. It's an interesting paradox really because you'll find that telling the truth actually makes you irresistibly attractive to a woman.

She Doesn't Have to Like the Outcome

A key to passing a woman's congruence test when her purpose for testing you is based on her *need* to *feel* your assertiveness is to realize that she doesn't have to like the outcome. If you go into a congruence test thinking that the only way to pass is by making her happy, you've already failed.

Think about it.

If you're overly concerned with making her happy, pleasing her, and ensuring that you avoid conflict at all costs you're not going to be able to respond from a position of masculine strength. To respond with masculine strength means you're responding from YOUR core values, standards, and beliefs, not hers.

Your woman really doesn't want you to be easily controlled by her, but that doesn't mean that she's not going to make an attempt just to test you. Once you understand that she doesn't have to like the outcome you'll be less tempted to hand over your nuts the minute she throws some conflict or disapproval your way.

Stick to Your Guns

Sticking to your guns is an idiom that means you refuse to compromise or change, despite criticism. It's a particularly useful phrase to keep in mind when you're faced with making a difficult decision that you wholeheartedly believe in, despite what your wife or girlfriend may think.

Sometimes you're going to have to make really tough decisions that your significant other simply will not agree with. Even after she's pleaded with you, presented her case, and argued, you must stick to your guns if you sincerely believe that your decision is for the greater good.

I remember a time leading up to a Black Friday sales event, my wife and I had discussed off and on the idea of purchasing a large, brand new LED television to place in the living room. Granted, we already had a smaller TV in our bedroom that we barely used, but for some reason we fancied the idea of getting a new, BIG TV so she could exercise to Zumba and on which I could watch my action movies.

Consider the fact that we refuse to pay for and therefore do not have cable or satellite television services because we're frugal when it comes to monthly expenses. On top of that, we could have moved the smaller TV into the living room and she could have just as easily used that to watch her exercise DVD's. But hey, why go small when we could spend our hard-earned cash for a TV that we "might" use more often?

Well, as you can see I was never completely sold on the idea of getting a new TV, but for some reason she got the impression that I was. As Black Friday came nearer she sent me a few shopping deals from online vendors, none of which I felt really excited about.

I'm the kind of man that makes purchases based on an item's quality as opposed to how "low" the price of something is. I rarely spend money just because of a "hot deal", but when I do I ensure that I buy the best possible quality for a price I deem fair. Black Friday or not, I wasn't about to spend money on something I wasn't sure I really even wanted in the first place, no matter how low the price might have been.

I pride myself on being unequivocally rational and perhaps even stubborn with how I spend money. It's a principle of mine that keeps me from being a slave to consumer culture. So with this *principle* of frugality firmly in mind, I decided that we didn't really need to spend money on a new TV.

My wife cajoled and argued but I didn't see the logic. I stuck to my guns and *reminded her of our financial and family goals*. Eventually, she figured out that I really didn't care too much about having a new television and realized that, at the moment, it wasn't THAT important to her either.

If she *really* wanted to watch Zumba, she could do so comfortably on the TV we already *owned*. In fact, later on in the day after I firmly told her *"No, we don't need it"* she seemed perfectly sweet and back to normal. She was thankful that I stood my ground and stuck to my beliefs, which actually increased her ability to trust in my judgment.

Curious isn't it? Could it possibly be that telling a woman "No" and manning up about your convictions, no matter how trivial they may seem, makes you *more* attractive to her? The world is filled with paradoxes, my friend. You won't know until you try it out for yourself.

On Being Too Stubborn

Obviously, this book was written for guys who struggle more on the side of being too passive with women. Therefore, the idea of sticking to your guns is designed to get you in the habit of being unwavering in your decisions. Although I believe that it's better to lean on the side of being *too* assertive as opposed to being *too* passive, as you develop the habit of sticking to your guns don't become so stubborn that you won't listen to reason.

I consider *sticking to your guns* analogous to being stubborn when it counts the most. Being too stubborn may make your wife or girlfriend feel as if she never has any say in any of the decisions that you do make. You must learn when something is worth arguing over and when it's better to find a win-win compromise.

Remember, a man makes his decisions to be congruent with his core values, his principles, and the greater good. If your woman or girlfriend presents you with sound reasons as to why changing your stance is for the greater good, take her judgment into consideration.

Don't be afraid of being "controlled" or "manipulated." Free your mind from the idea of win-lose outcomes and learn to see the forest for the trees. A wise man knows when to remain steadfast and when to change his course in order to benefit not just himself, but those under his care as well.

Pushing Through Her Intimidation

If you say something cocky or even audacious with a woman and she pauses, frowns, and gives you a glaring gaze as if she's thinking, *"Did he just say that to me?"* do you back down and apologize or maintain your cool through her intimidation?

Maintaining your cool through her intimidation increases her attraction to you as you dominate her space with your certainty. Apologizing, backing down, or reacting in a panicked way ruins the illusion. (Note: If you back down it's obvious that your previous boldness WAS in fact, an illusion. Refusing to back down means that it WASN'T an illusion in the first place.)

As a married man, if I say naughty things to my wife implying that she must please me sexually in some fashion and I back down after she gives me the *"And just who do you think you are?"* look, chances are I'm not going to get what I want. Why? The reason is simple: Because I lacked *certainty*.

Men with irrational confidence subconsciously communicate their confidence in a way that causes a woman to feel a sense of his certainty. Women are highly intuitive and respond unconsciously to a man's *behavior*. Your actions truly do speak louder than your words, as it's the subtle things a woman picks up about you that cue whether or not you really believe what you're trying to sell her.

Your tone of voice, body language, and posturing reveal to her how certain you are about whether or not you're going to get what you want. Women love men who are certain that they're going to get exactly what they want.

It's a shift in your thinking that must take place in order to convey an attitude of certainty. But just like anything else in life, you'll believe it the more you actually *act* the part. One of your brain's functions is to close the gap of incongruence between what you believe about yourself and how you actually behave. Because of this, over time your mind will work to reinforce the belief that you're a man of certainty once you consistently display those behaviors.

Stop Agreeing with Everything

Have you ever met a man who always agreed with everything his wife said and did? Regardless of what she says or does is right or wrong, he agrees without question and would rather cut off his eyelids than to disagree with her. He's a "yes" man, and you, my friend, do not want to be a "yes" man.

Imagine going to see a movie with your wife or girlfriend, one that you totally enjoyed but she completely despised. You walk out of the theater beaming from ear-to-ear, reciting some of the movie's best lines while raving about how much you loved the film. She, on the other hand, hated every minute of the film and has no qualms about voicing her dissatisfaction. A man who agrees to a fault might experience an interaction like this:

Him: "That movie was awesome. I loved every minute of it."

Her: "Really? I kind of thought it sucked. The dialogue was cheesy and the action was way over-the-top."

Him: "Hmm. You have a good point. Well, I guess it wasn't THAT good."

What? Are you kidding me? He just said that he totally enjoyed the film now he's changing his stance? Somebody give this guy an opinion because he obviously doesn't have one of his own. Seriously, as contrived as that conversation may seem there are men out there that have a desperate, nagging need to agree with everything a woman says and thinks.

If you're dating, it's times like this when a woman may test you just to see if you'll stand by your opinion. She wants to know that you can be honest with *yourself* and disagree with her, but still get along with her. She wants to know that you have your own preferences and you're not afraid to make them known. This is the sort of behavior that earns the respect and adoration of a good woman.

To revisit our little example, here's how a man with a backbone and an opinion would respond:

Him: "That movie was awesome. I loved every

minute of it."

Her: "Really? I kind of thought it sucked. The dialogue was cheesy and the action was way over-the-top."

Him: "Well, while you're entitled to your opinion. I still say it was a spectacular film."

The example above was a simple and respectful response to a difference of opinion. On the other hand, if you are known to tease you can be a bit more cocky and humorous with her:

Him: "That movie was awesome. I loved every minute of it."

Her: "Really? I kind of thought it sucked. The dialogue was cheesy and the action was way over-the-top."

Him: "Wow. And here I was thinking that my girlfriend/wife had taste. Oh well, I guess I'm the cultured one in the relationship."

*Her: "I have taste!" *...as she laughs and hits him playfully**

Now, I'm sure there are some married guys out there that would rather just agree with their wives about a particular matter than to hear her nag him about his opinion. While I understand how exasperating it can be to have to endure the rants of a woman who disagrees with your viewpoint, I can't help but wonder what the long-term effects of always deferring your opinion to hers may have on a relationship.

While I'm not advocating that you argue with a woman over every single thing, I still believe that it's better for a man to be a challenge to his woman from time to time. The habit of rolling over and playing dead with your opinions won't earn you her respect, and it certainly won't make her feel attracted to you in the long-run.

Conflict crafts a man's character; therefore, avoiding it entirely won't make you any better. If you've been unconsciously complying with your woman's opinion for years, it may be time to shake things up. If she has the habit of giving you a hard time just because you disagree, make it clear that you're *entitled* to your own opinion and that you're not interested in defending your preferences. Here's an example of this in action:

Her: "Honey, what did you think of today's sermon?"

Him: "I thought it was abysmal."

Her: "Are you kidding me? That was one of Pastor Greg's best sermons. You really didn't like it?"

Him: "No. I think he meanders off topic too much."

Her: "I don't believe this. You really don't like anything Pastor Greg teaches. You're an idiot if you think…"

Him: "Look, you asked me my opinion and I gave it. If you don't like hearing the truth from me I suggest you think twice before asking what I think."

Beautifully done. This is what you call *setting boundaries* as you're making it quite clear that you're entitled to your own opinion and if she doesn't like it she has the choice not to ask in the first place. On the other hand, you can nuke any further inquiries of your opinion by providing a clear reason earlier on in the conversation.

Here's how it might look:

Her: "Honey, what did you think of today's sermon?"

Him: "I thought it was abysmal. I prefer Pastor Fred's sermons. That man has guts. He speaks his mind and isn't afraid to say the truth. Pastor Greg supplicates to the crowd too much."

Her: "Are you kidding me? That was one of Pastor Greg's best sermons."

Him: "Well, you're entitled to your own opinion, love."

Women who are a bit more feisty and quick-tongued may not let you get off as easy as the women in these examples. So what does a man do when he has voiced his opinion but is now being goaded into an argument? Easy, he must refuse to argue. If you've stood by your convictions and she still thinks it's imperative that she explains why you are wrong, simply say, *"I will not argue with you about this."* Say it firmly and lovingly then change the topic altogether.

Don't be afraid to speak your mind just because a woman might try to force her opinion on you. It's important for two adults in an adult relationship to treat each other like adults. Be honest with your opinions and be clear with your boundaries. She may disagree with you and even show signs of annoyance at your bluntness, but a good woman will cherish the fact that you're not afraid to be honest and firm with her.

Seek Her Advice Not Her Approval

A married man will often need to consult with his wife before making certain decisions, especially when these decisions affect the family. Even a man who has a serious girlfriend may find himself seeking her counsel when he's faced with a particularly perplexing dilemma. That's fine, and there's nothing wrong with needing to gain the advice or even the support of your woman in certain situations.

When I say to "seek her advice not her approval", what I mean is that it's important for a man to understand the difference between living based on his principles and living based on a woman's approval. If most of the decisions you make come down to whether or not your choice will "upset" your woman, you're not living based on principles and your values.

A man without principles, without values, stands for nothing. Always looking to a woman to see if you're making the right decision is detrimental to your development as a man and it can cripple your happiness. The need to please is a sickness that must be eradicated, and unless a situation arises that forces a man to free himself from the need for a woman's approval he may spend the rest of his life being guided, perhaps subconsciously, by the most influential women in his life, i.e. girlfriend, wife, mother, etc.

Now, I understand that all this should be considered in context. For example, wanting to spend the evening playing pool with your friends does not require a counsel of two unless the decision to do so interferes with previously arranged plans made by you and your wife or girlfriend.

If it does not interfere, there is a clear difference between asking her if you can play pool with your friends tonight and telling her that you're going to play pool with your friends. If you *value* your male friendships, it's important that the woman you choose understands this. Spending time with them is something that you *value*, it is significant to you and therefore it is a part of who you are.

There's nothing wrong with seeking your woman's advice, especially if she's more skilled or knowledgeable in a certain area. A wise man seeks advice and makes his decision once he feels confident that he's well informed. On the other hand, a foolish man doesn't seek advice while a sucker-of-a-man seeks both advice and a woman's approval.

There will be times when a woman's advice will prove invaluable to you because of her skill, knowledge, or intuition. But not every decision you make will require her input, even less her approval. Learn the difference and be your own man, one guided by principles and values, rather than the approval of women.

Choosing to live based on your values isn't something that you need to gain a woman's approval for. When it comes to your principles and values, you must develop a take it or leave it approach when dealing with others. That's not to say that you should always be selfish and uncompromising in your ways (especially if you're interested in cultivating a relationship). But when you do choose to compromise, it's because of a *conscious* choice rather than a subconscious habit of gaining a woman's approval first. In short, your values and principles should always be your default.

But how does all this relate to a woman testing you? Simple. During the dating phase and in the early stages of a relationship, a woman may test to see just how compliant you are with HER plans and desires. This is clearly a play for power, and some women, especially those who have a habit of getting their way with men, will test you to see if her plans, needs, desires, and wants are more important to you than your plans, needs, desires, and wants.

Her test will seek to outmaneuver you, perhaps through guilt, and make you choose what she wants over what you want. What some women do, albeit subconsciously, is TRAIN men to be dependent on their approval before they make a decision. To her, once she's programmed you, she will favorably grant you a "yes" or "no" to the decision you want to make once the outcome does not interfere with her own happiness.

Now you may be thinking, "What's so wrong with wanting to make her happy? Why wouldn't she say no to something that would make her unhappy if I did it?" Excellent questions my friend, and I will answer you. If most or all the decisions you make are based on whether or not she'll be "happy" with it, you're making yourself a second-class citizen in your own relationship.

Just to remind you, the whole point of this book is to illustrate how women will test you to see if you're a man they can trust to lead and love them or if you're a man they can dominate and manipulate. If she tests you and you constantly submit to her because you don't want her to be "unhappy", you're seriously jeopardizing your ability to lead her effectively.

Keep in mind that as a leader not every decision you make is supposed to make her happy. And as an individual, you cannot maintain your own happiness if you constantly suppress your own needs just to make the woman happy. Don't become an empty shell of a man by being an approval seeking, woman-pleasing male.

A woman WILL test you to see how much she can get away with. So if you don't train her to realize that not every decision you make will make her happy (but it will make you a better man and therefore a better boyfriend or husband) expect one day to find yourself gradually dying inside as the firm grasp of her fingers around your nuts slowly drain the last remnants of masculine strength from your very being.

I know, I know, I'm such a poet.

Making Decisions for Her

I've noticed something very interesting that women do if they aren't already decided on something. Sometimes your woman is going to want you to make a decision for her but she's not going to tell you, *"Honey, I want you to make this decision for me."* Instead of coming right out and asking you to make a decision for her she's going to mask her indecisiveness in a question or statement.

What's worse is that if you already have the habit of passing the buck back to her by trying to make her decide she'll grow contemptuous of your inability to make a decision. These, my friend, are probably the most often failed tests men face in relationships simply because they're engineered to IMMEDIATELY separate a self-assured man who leads and an approval-seeking wussy who would rather not be bothered.

If you have a bad habit of always asking your woman what she wants she'll eventually start throwing tests your way specifically designed to compel you to make more decisions, decisions that incorporate her as well. In these instances, what she really wants is for you to take her by the hand and lead her. She really doesn't even care *what* you decide as long as you make a decision and stand by it.

Now, there will be times you'll have to include her in the decision-making process, that's fine. But in these certain situations in which she's subconsciously testing your decision-making mettle she'd rather abdicate the responsibility of choosing to you.

So how do you know when a woman is testing your decision-making ability? Easy. Look at the subtext behind her question or statement. The statement or question is going to be so simple that to you, it doesn't make sense why she's even telling or asking you. It's almost as if she can handle it herself and that she's just trying to *annoy* you. When you feel a twinge of annoyance, irritation, or if the phrase, *"Why is she telling me this?"* pops into your mind, there's a good chance something is up.

For example, here's a famous one that men all around the world have been failing since the dawn of time:

"I'm hungry."

Seriously. If a woman has ever told you that she's hungry she wants you to make a decision. If you're married and there's a ton of food in the fridge yet she sits next to you on the couch as you watch the game and opens her mouth to say, *"Honey, I'm hungry"* something deeper is going on. Two derivatives of this are *"What are we having for dinner?"* or *"What would you like for me to cook?"*

You probably love your woman's cooking so you really don't care what she decides to cook for dinner, but that's not the point. If she's the type of woman who seeks out male leadership she *prefers* it if you made the decision.

Best response: *"I'm hungry too. Let's grab a bite. Put on your shoes."* If she asks where you're going keep her in suspense until you figure out where you'd like to eat. This is a great comeback because it adds in a bit of adventure as she goes along for the ride.

Another response: *"I'm hungry too. I want steaks tonight. I love your steaks."* Again, make a decision. If she offers up another suggestion, that's okay. You've already aced her test and now she's more than willing to play ball with you and come to an agreement about the evening's dinner.

Years of experience has taught me that sometimes it doesn't even matter what she eats so long as you either offer her a few suggestions or take her by the hand and go grab a bite together. On the other hand, if she says that she's hungry and you're not you can say: *"Well, I'm not. Grab a snack for now. We'll go grab something when the game is done. My treat."* Add in a wolfish wink and a sly grin and she'll be more than satisfied to follow your lead.

Do More, Ask Less

A great way to relate with your woman from a position of leadership is to take charge and initiate without her permission. Instead of constantly supplicating and asking for her approval, be a man and act accordingly to meet her needs as well as yours. For example, if your girlfriend complains about her muscles being sore you can either ask her if she wants a massage or you can *take charge* and tell her that you're going to give her one.

A true leader makes mistakes of ambition rather than mistakes of apathy. If she really doesn't want a massage she'll tell you after the fact. Either way she'll appreciate your initiative as opposed to growing contemptuous of your supplication had you asked her if she required one instead. Yes, women are even looking for you to lead like a man in areas as subtle as this one.

Remember, be decisive, be mysterious, tease her a little, but make room for her suggestions if she *wants* to provide input. Being more decisive and taking initiative is far more desirable to a woman than waiting for her to decide and always asking what she wants. Just be aware that bullying a woman into doing what you want to do isn't the solution either.

So if you find that over time she'd like to have more input in the decision-making process go ahead and make room for her suggestions. It's much better to have a woman ask you to include her in your leadership than for her to grow contemptuous of your supplication.

Sleeping on the Couch

It is my firm opinion that no man should ever have to be relegated to sleeping on the couch because his wife is upset or angry with him. I spent my youth watching sitcoms and shows where husbands with ticked off wives spent their lonely nights sprawled out on uncomfortable couches. Even as a young boy these scenes never sat well with me. They literally made me uncomfortable and I began to question this strange and foreign dynamic.

If your wife makes you sleep on the couch or in another room after a fight or argument you're not the one wearing the pants in the relationship. Even if you *choose* to sleep anywhere else than your own paid-for bed, you're signaling that your mate can coerce you, the alpha bear, out of your nice, warm den. Unless violence may ensue (which should never even be in question) a man should sleep in his own bed even if his wife is angry.

If there's something you should have apologized for and you did already, you should rest easy on your pillow knowing that you did what you had to do. Let smoke blow out of her ears all night as you snore the night away right next to her. I find it hard to believe that a "good husband" would sleep on the couch just so his angry wife can get a good night's sleep.

Only a man convinced of his own righteousness is going to get a good night's sleep next to a fuming, angry woman. So assuming she's upset for something ridiculous and unreasonable, it's much better to stand your ground and enjoy the comfort of your side of the bed (the side she rolls over to anyway).

CHAPTER 6:
Being the Rock a Woman Needs

Don't Be Who You're Supposed to Be

A lot of guys who suffer in their relationships with women seem to have one thing in common. They burn a ton of energy trying to do *the right thing* to make a woman happy. Nothing frustrates a woman more than a man who's always trying to monitor his words and actions just to keep her on the level and pleased.

In the short-term, this may seem like a good plan. I mean, why wouldn't it work? If she throws some drama your way, you can just say or do something completely predictable, passive, and non-confrontational just to keep things the way they are. Unfortunately, over the long-term this is a recipe for relationship failure.

Obviously, if she's throwing some drama your way it's because she wants something from you. And chances are the very thing that she wants is for you to say or do something completely unexpected. She might be looking for something different, something better than what she's been experiencing with you, something *authentic* and one-hundred percent *masculine*. But what do most men do instead? They opt for the easy way out, and give her something she's seen before, something uninspired, something vanilla.

Here's the thing. When a woman feels uncertain about you she may purposefully push your buttons in a manner that will result in you responding negatively. In short, she's actually setting you up for failure. Deep down inside, she hopes that you will prove her suspicions wrong and pass her test with flying colors. But in the event that you do fail, she's already decided that her attempts to ascertain who you are will only intensify as time goes on.

If a man spends most of his time trying to do everything *he thinks* a woman wants him to do, he's already failed. When a woman tests you consciously or subconsciously, she wants to get a sense of the REAL you. If you're always saying what you think she wants you to say or doing what you think she wants you to do just to make her happy and *please* her, she'll never get a true feeling for your authentic masculine nature.

Because of this, she'll keep on fabricating situations designed to force the real you out. If you don't know who you are (because you're always trying to be someone else to please her) she certainly won't know who you are. And for a woman, she's not going to ease up until she convinces you to drop the mask and just be the man YOU want to be.

As with anything related to handling a woman's congruence tests, it's all about the mindset. If you approach your interactions with a woman from a "no risk" mindset, you're free to respond from a place of authenticity. In other words, you're free to be the man you are and act with integrity.

Having a mindset that there is no "right" or "wrong" in how you interact with your woman is powerful because it sets you free from trying to please her every time you relate with her. When you're not trying to gain anything and you don't fear losing anything (her respect, love, affection, etc.) your interactions will contain much more integrity. A man's integrity is something that a woman can ultimately rely on.

Have Your Own Standards

Sometimes a woman is going to constantly test you just to see if you have any standards of your own. Taken a bit farther, a woman might even test you just to see if the standards that you do have are ones in which you're willing to defend. Many a relationship quarrel has been started all because a man did or said something that his woman deemed below her standards.

In these sorts of dynamics, women like this tend to think that if something isn't done their way, it's wrong. They tend to think that their way of doing things is the best way of doing it, and that anything different is simply inferior. Some women who act like this tend to be spoiled rotten, therefore they act disrespectfully.

All this is due to the fact that the men in their lives *allow* them to get away with atrocious behavior. Women like this have a habit of treating the men in their lives like children; berating them every time they don't perform to mommy's standard. This isn't healthy in an adult relationship, and it's certainly not conducive to long-term relationship happiness.

Sadly, you really can't blame her. If a woman continually tests a man by giving him a hell of a hard time every time he does something "wrong", and he responds by trying to do it the "right" way (her way), then she'll NEVER be satisfied. You read that right.

Even if you eventually do everything she wants the "right way" (her way), she'll continue to invent new and more complex challenges in order to showcase your vast inferiority. So if doing it "right" won't solve the problem, what will? Simple. Do it "better." And by "better", I mean do it YOUR way…except with assertiveness and confidence.

The next time your woman gives you flack about a chore, task, etc. that didn't meet her standards, stand your ground and let her know that that's the way you like doing it and that's the way you're going to continue to do it. Develop a take it or leave it approach to this kind of situation. If she doesn't like the way you do things, she can either learn to like it, do it herself and never ask you again, or keep quiet about it altogether. As a man, you must define your standards and then *train* your woman to respect the way you do things.

Now, I'm assuming the way you do things still gets the job done, and done well. If you can honestly say that your woman nitpicks with the way you do things simply because you didn't do it her way, then I beseech you my friend to take a stand and say "no more."

A woman wants you to have your own set of standards and she wants you to enforce them, not necessarily on her but on yourself. If you don't have any standards, she's going to test you by enforcing hers upon you. If you have standards but you don't respect yourself enough to enforce them, she's going to test you by nitpicking and second-guessing just about every decision you make.

Women who act like this tend to believe that the world revolves around them. Some women simply need to realize that her man's standards are just as important as her own. Yes, in some situations her way of handling things might be superior to yours, but the dynamic I'm referring to is one where a woman consistently berates her man for his "mistakes" or way of doing things.

If your wife or girlfriend acts this way, it's important that she somehow becomes aware of the fact that in an adult relationship both partners must be able to express their standards comfortably. If your woman insists on expressing and enforcing her standards above yours, you definitely don't have an adult relationship. It's unquestionably more of a mother-son type dynamic at work. You are not a child and your wife is not your mother.

Be Firm or Have Fun with Her

I can find a ton of examples of a woman unconsciously testing her man's standards, but what follows is a very simple one. Let's say that just about every time you're going somewhere with your wife or girlfriend she has a problem with where and how you park the car. You're having a good time with her throughout the car ride, but as you reach your destination you get that little twinge in the gut of your stomach because you know without a shadow of a doubt that she's going to have something to say about your choice and method of parking. It's not that she's disabled and you park too far or that you always park in the sun; she just always seems to express her displeasure whenever you park, no matter where or how you do it.

So lo and behold, you park the car and yet again she asks you a question you've heard far too often, *"Why are you parking here?"* Now, prior to the knowledge I've imparted to you in this book you may have opted for the non-confrontational approach and try to *explain* YOUR decision to her.

Even worse, you've probably even trained yourself to ask her, *"Where should we park, honey?"* or *"Are you happy with the way I'm doing it?"* If she's being unreasonable when she questions your way of doing things, changing your way of doing things won't make her happy.

Now, prior to this book you may have thought that as long as you don't confront her questioning, eventually she'll learn to ease up and just let you decide to park where and how you'd like to. WRONG. In a situation like this where she's developed the habit of questioning the little decisions you make *without reason*, it's time that you took a stand and confronted her. It's times like this when some men wise up and unconsciously realize that the only way to put an end (or at least draw attention) to such behavior is to do the counterintuitive thing – stand up for your standards.

So next time, when she's giving you the business about your parking prowess (or whatever else for that matter), look her firmly in the eye and with a cocky grin tell her, *"Listen, you're not driving, I am. I parked here because I want to."* Those last four words are particularly powerful, especially if you've been playing into her game for most of the relationship.

On the other hand, you can get even more specific with her and defend your decision without really defending it. For example, if she asks, *"Why did you park so far?"* with that same old cocky grin you can reply, *"Because I enjoy taking long walks with my wife."*

Naturally, your mileage may vary with that last one but the science behind it is sound. If she gives you the business about the way you do things, stand your ground firmly or with a hint of fun. Make a habit out of it and she'll eventually get the message.

Keep in mind that if you've been a "nice guy" your whole life, a firm, assertive reply like the first one I mentioned above might make you cringe. The thought of saying such a thing to the woman you love might make you feel uncomfortable and downright nasty. What you're experiencing is discomfort, and it's a natural part of masculine transformation.

Trust me; if nothing you do makes your woman happy no matter how hard you try, you're simply trying too hard to make her happy. Sometimes, all a woman wants is for her man to take a stand for his standards.

Own It and Move On

One of the most powerful responses you can give to a woman who insists on calling out your mistakes and shortcomings is to actually own up to them and move on. Ever seen the movie *8 Mile*, starring rapper Eminem? The big climax of the film shows Eminem's character, Jimmy "B-Rabbit" Smith Jr., in a vicious freestyle rap battle against rappers from a rival gang.

During the course of the film, because of the rival gang, Jimmy gets beat up, screwed over, and his girlfriend cheats on him. Armed with the fact that the rival gang he's battling against in the rap tournament has totally humiliated him, he does the only thing he can do to take the venom out of his enemy's stinger – he owns it.

Instead of waiting for the rival gang to use all of the humiliating truths about his life to insult him on stage he preemptively addresses them in his freestyle. In fact, w*ithout shame* he acknowledges his lower-class upbringings and all of the humiliations inflicted upon him by the rival gang right before insulting the gang's leader, Papa Doc. The result? Papa Doc no longer has any ammunition to "diss" Jimmy with in his rap. Unexpectedly deflated, Papa Doc scurries off stage and leaves with the rest of his gang.

I referenced this film because of the valuable lesson within it. You can take the venom out of your own screw-ups, humiliations, and shortcomings by being unashamedly forthright with yourself and therefore with your woman. You'll sometimes find yourself being called out for less-than-ideal behavior by the woman you love.

It's at those times she'll see just how well you can handle criticism, especially when it's necessary criticism designed to help you become a better man. Instead of taking what she says personally or feeling ashamed of something you said or did, own up to it and move on. Take the venom out of her stinger, especially if she has the habit of teasing you about your shortcomings.

For example, let's say that you're so socially awkward that it causes your wife or girlfriend to criticize you when you're both alone. What do you say when she criticizes you and calls out your blundering behavior? You "own it", perhaps a bit like this:

"You know, you're right. I could have handled that a lot better."

Or…

"Yeah, I'll be honest, it's not one of my noblest qualities."

Or…

"I'll admit that I do struggle with _____ at

times."

The above statements are simple, straightforward, and most importantly, shameless. And assuming she's not consciously going out of her way to tear into you, statements like these should be more than enough to disarm her.

Don't try to deny it if you know it's true and don't try to explain the facts away. When necessary, it's a good strategy to showcase your insecurity or weakness so no one else has a chance to put a spotlight on it. Accepting it *without shame* is the key to maintaining a frame of authority even when you're being called out for subpar or embarrassing behavior. And using simple phrases that demonstrate this strong self-acceptance is all that's needed to keep her on her toes and off of your back.

On Being Honest and Vulnerable

My biggest problem with some of the relationship advice out there for men has to do with the idea that a man must never do anything that might hint at his insecurities when relating with women. There's this notion that being vulnerable with the woman you love (or are growing to love) can backfire on you. While being an insecure wussy around a woman will only make her feel contempt, voicing your heart-felt discomfort with honesty will earn her respect.

I had to mention this because it's very easy to fall prey to the idea that you MUST show a woman that you're self-assured if she tests you or if she presents you with a situation that involves your decision-making. There's nothing wrong with illustrating confidence through indifference once that confidence is coming from a place of honesty.

It's another thing entirely to feel sincere discomfort or uneasiness and choose to bottle it inside because you don't want to appear weak and insecure. Many men have made bad decisions so as not to appear "weak" to a woman.

For example, let's say that your girlfriend's coworker is getting married and she has invited her to her bachelorette party. Your girlfriend then approaches you and tells you what the evening is going to look like. She clearly informs you that there will be copious amounts of alcohol and male strippers involved, and she truly wants to know if she has your blessing to go.

Now, a man who thinks that this is some sort of test (and it might be depending on the situation) might decide to show her that he doesn't feel insecure or threatened at the idea of his sweet, good girl being surrounded by drunken females and opportunistic male strippers. Of course, if he isn't insecure about it and feels completely confident in his woman's ability to make sound decisions then that's one thing.

On the other hand, let's say that while you do trust your girlfriend implicitly, you don't trust the situation or her more hedonistic coworkers. If that's the case it makes more sense to be honest with her and tell her exactly how you feel. Tell her, *"No, I don't want you to go. I don't want you in a situation that might force you to behave in ways that would make me uncomfortable."*

This is powerful, vulnerable, and most importantly, honest. You're not putting on a front by telling her, *"Sure, you can go, just behave yourself"* all the while you can't function properly knowing that she might be peer pressured into making questionable decisions.

A similar situation happened to a brother of mine. He told his girlfriend how he honestly felt about a very questionable social situation she was about to get herself into. She took heed to his leadership and later admitted to him that she was hoping he'd express his disapproval. She actually admitted to him that though she would have gone had he given his blessing, she was testing him to see if he actually cared enough about her and their relationship to tell her "NO." Wow.

Women tend to test a man's level of commitment by gauging his desire to protect her and to preserve her sexual interest. Put another way, if a woman isn't convinced that you're interested in her enough to guard her from other potential men, she might test your resolve in order to gain reassurance. Can she trust you to make sound decisions and take a firm stance even when she *seems* determined to have her own way?

Remember, a quality woman wants your honesty even if it does reveal your discomfort. In these sorts of situations, showing your concern for her and the integrity of your relationship is far more attractive to her than trying to *act* indifferent.

Acknowledging Your Threshold – A Man's True Strength

Being a "strong" man gets a lot of lip service in society, especially when it comes to topics of dating and relating with women. You may research topics about being an "alpha male" and how it's important for a man to dominate and prove he can withstand the challenges of life.

While all these things are true on some level, the idea of a man's true strength and where it comes from never gets fully addressed. Now, I'll admit that I'm not the wisest man on the planet but this very notion of what a man's true strength is can change the way you view the world.

To put it simply, for a man to display true strength he needs to *be honest with how much he's willing to tolerate*. Knowing what you're willing to put up with, endure, and persevere through when dealing with people is vitally important to being a man who possesses both guts and integrity.

If you are afraid to be honest about your limits and your weaknesses, you're going to have a heck of a time setting boundaries with people and expressing your needs and desires to others, especially women.

You'll find that men who think that true strength comes from *pretending* to be strong in the face of conflict often care far too much about what others *think* of them than for how they feel about themselves. To them, it's better to be liked, to be seen as being strong, or to be honored than to stop and say, *"No. I've had enough. I don't like this. Stop it or I'm going to remove myself from this situation."* They'd rather be seen as men who can "take it" or who can "handle it" as opposed to admitting that like other men, they have insecurities, limitations, and thresholds for pain.

How do you know if your interactions with others stem from a place of true strength and authenticity? Easy. When someone does something you don't like, something that *really* gets under your skin, do you speak up about your dislike or do you keep it inside and try to be a good sport? When you feel as if your boundaries are being crossed and it's clearly making you uncomfortable, do you keep those feelings to yourself or are you honest with others?

A man can be vulnerable and yet still be confident. Being a man of strength is more about being honest with yourself and others and less about trying to prove that you're a strong guy with superior emotional fortitude. Read that last sentence again.

Women and people in general, will connect with you on a much deeper level when you're vulnerable with them. And through this vulnerability, this honest display of humanness, you earn their respect. I'm not talking about anything necessarily deep here. You can be honest about something as simple as jokes being made about someone you care about.

For example, you may not be comfortable with the way your coworkers talk about each other's wives/girlfriends. For them it may seem like harmless fun, but to you it comes off as disrespectful and low-grade behavior that you want no part of. The more they do it, the more it bothers you.

And because you want to be a good sport and you *believe* that you have no influence over their behavior you automatically keep silent. So you continue to endure and suffer as their behavior slowly grows on you until you too become just "one of the boys." The alternative? You stick to your principles and remain honest with yourself and your coworkers.

If you abhor the fact that they often make fun of each other's wives/girlfriends, speak your mind and let the chips fall where they may. If they respect you they'll refrain from involving you. If they don't respect you they'll continue to do it around you, which means that you must consciously limit your interactions with them.

Who cares if they think you are oversensitive or you're not being a good sport? You have standards and principles that you're unwilling to compromise for anyone. The people worth having in your life are the ones who *respect* your boundaries. Limit or dissolve your interactions with those who continually cross your boundaries. Be honest with what you're willing to tolerate and be willing to walk away. It's that simple.

Yes, being vulnerable and honest about what you're willing to put up with might make you unpopular with some. Heck, they may even begin insulting you behind your back. But those who do like you will be highly attracted to your authenticity, both men and women.

If you are single, you'll make yourself highly attractive to the RIGHT woman. If you're already in a relationship, you'll find passing a woman's tests to be ridiculously easier since you're unafraid to assert your boundaries with her.

Leading Through Vulnerability

No matter how you relate with a woman, you must never, ever, stop leading. It's not something you just turn off because you'd rather be a nurtured, protected mama's boy again. If you need to get advice from her you go to her from a frame of leadership, like a powerful corporate president and CEO getting insight from his vice president.

Even if you need her support, encouragement, or comfort you go to her with the understanding that she's fulfilling your needs not "filling in your missing pieces."

You're better off saying something like, *"Honey, I need to get something off my chest. Let's talk for a minute"* rather than complaining or whining to her straight out the gate like a mama's boy. Remember, it's not what you do but how you do it. Context is everything.

There will be times when our wives and girlfriends will see us at our lowest and we'll need their emotional support. Some guys lean on the extreme and think that they're not supposed to show a woman any weakness. This isn't human, and it's not realistic.

In my opinion, there's nothing wrong with a man being vulnerable with the woman he loves. Being vulnerable is healthy for cultivating intimacy in a relationship. The problem arises when your displays of vulnerability *consistently* creep out without you wanting them to. It shows a lack of self-control (and probably testosterone).

It's better for a man to be in control of his emotions more often than not. You want to be in a position of control so that you can open up the doors to your soul yourself and let a woman in than to have them constantly swung open by every challenge or distress life throws your way. By letting her in, you're leading.

Some women even prefer tearing those layers away themselves. They love a stoic man who approaches life with a stiff upper lip. But if you always run to her the minute your emotions get the best of you you're not giving her a chance to run to your aid instead. Give her the opportunity to tend to her wounded hero.

Don't always run to your wife or girlfriend first every time life throws you a challenge. A woman may question your ability to be her source of strength and encouragement if you're always relying on her alone for strength. Because she needs you to be her rock you must ensure that your reserve of masculine strength is never fully depleted.

This is why having a male mentor, father figure, brother, or group of male friends to talk your issues out with is so useful. It's a better alternative to always relying on your woman as your only source of encouragement. Having a brotherhood of good men whose insights you can trust is invaluable.

Going to a man/men to problem solve will help to refine you as a man, while sharing your experiences will help you to realize that you're not alone, no matter how isolated you may actually feel. If you've been looking for a way to increase your masculine maturity having a guy or group of guys to talk things out with is a great resource.

Letting Go of Anger and Resentment

If you're determined to make a relationship work no matter what, you need to reframe the way you look at a woman's tests, learn how to respond effectively, and let go of any anger and resentment. If you struggle with feelings of pride, letting go of your self-righteous anger may prove especially difficult. Even so, it's absolutely necessary to learn how to let things go if you're going to get along well with women (and anyone else for that matter). It's always easier to build a better future once you are not weighed down by the past.

If you're reading this and you realize that your wife or girlfriend has been testing you for years and that failing to pass those tests has resulted in years of ongoing conflict and frustration, you may experience strong feelings of anger and bitterness. That's a part of the process.

The next step is to let go of it and see things in a new light. Realize that with this new knowledge you can actually enjoy a more harmonious and fulfilling relationship with the woman you love. New beginnings are always possible once you don't allow years of bitterness to define the man you want to be and the relationship you want to build.

If you truly accept the fact that most women don't realize that they test men in the ways I mention in this book, you'll have a much easier time showing forgiveness and not taking things personally. It's difficult to hold something against someone if you realized that they really didn't know any better.

Of course, I'm not advocating that you let a woman's negative behavior slide and become her doormat. You must forgive but you must also set strong boundaries and assert yourself. Keep in mind that forgiveness is an attitude of mind that greatly affects your behavior. You truly become a better man for it as it changes your attitude from a fragile wussy-of-a-man into that of a man of grace, benevolence, and magnanimity. The former makes you think and act like a victim; the latter like a man with poise and authority. Be a man of poise and authority.

Working Towards the Greater Good

I honestly believe that the best way to love another human being is by acknowledging our own humanity first and foremost. As human beings we all have rough edges, flaws, and ways about us that are less than divine. So what's our saving grace?

We are capable of seeing the good in ourselves and in others. We can dwell on the things we despise about each other or we can seek to inspire the good in others. In reality, relationships aren't about games and manipulation, they're about healing; healing that one can only experience through deep intimacy with another human being.

Even as men, without first acknowledging our own hurts, insecurities, weaknesses, and needs it's impossible for us to find true intimacy with a woman. This is one of the reasons some men have difficulty committing to a single woman.

Beyond the desire for sexual variety, the inability to trust a woman limits the amount of intimacy a man can experience with the fairer sex. Being afraid of being hurt can make a man coarse and defensive. Instead of loving a woman from a place of vulnerability he ends up loving her in a way that protects his ego.

Loving a woman, through her tests and irrational behavior requires a fearless heart. Therefore, a man should approach loving a woman from a place of egoless-ness. Every interaction you have with a woman should not be an exercise in trying to get her to meet your needs. Yes, you have needs that need meeting but mature, adult relationships are more about the joy of giving.

Once you enter a romantic relationship with a woman you have unconsciously decided to take on the responsibility of male leadership. From that point on, one of your jobs is to ensure that the decisions you make for the both of you are for the greater good.

Whether it means breaking up with your girlfriend because you know she's not right for you (or vice versa), taking the initiative to go to marriage counseling, or setting firm boundaries with a woman, it's important to look beyond your selfish desires and hers so that you can move towards the greater good. If you want to make better decisions in your interactions with women, master your own emotions so that you never find yourself afraid of hers.

Being a man is a gift so revel in your masculinity but don't let it rule you. Let your power stem from a place of compassion and a desire to help others better themselves. You cannot do this if you're always being "nice." A harmless man is an unhappy, ineffectual creature. A man needs challenge in his life. He requires conflict, something to push against to test his mettle and make him better. So don't fear a woman's tests – revel in them.

A woman wants a man who leads with compassion and who loves with passion. The kind of man who has found his path in life and he won't be shaken from it – this is what a good woman really wants.

Sometimes it's Not About You

Sometimes, for reasons beyond the understanding of us mere mortals called men, a woman will just go King

Kong waking-up-in-New-York crazy and you'll be the unfortunate victim that experiences it. When that happens, the only thing you can do to avoid getting caught up in her rampage is to sit back, reflect, and tell yourself (in your head), *"This has absolutely nothing to do with me."*

Sometimes, she's just going to have a bad day and it's not going to be your fault. Sometimes, someone is going to say or do something to make her feel insecure, and it's not going to be your fault. I know I've struggled with this before, especially when you really have a desire to make your woman happy.

Don't allow yourself to suffer just because she's suffering from insecurity. You can empathize with her and show her compassion, but you don't have to suffer with her by thinking that it's always up to you to make her happy.

Sometimes your woman will test you because of an insecurity that was triggered by something external to your relationship. When this happens, don't internalize it. If you habitually internalize every occurrence of her unhappiness, irrationality, or disrespect, you are only setting yourself up for failure and resentment. Sometimes she's going to lose her mind or say something to get under your skin just because…and in those moments, it's important to remember that it's not always about you.

As I've probably already mentioned a thousand times in this book, one of the worse things you can do when a woman gets like this is to get caught up in her emotions and allow her insecurities to poison, yes, POISON your perception and cripple your ability to relate with and respond to her.

If you act like a wussy every time she has a psychotic moment, a minor (or major) meltdown, or a visit from the ghost of Christmas crazy, you'll continue to fail her tests and miss opportunities to develop intimacy. Sometimes, it's not about you. So being a self-centered, self-conscious, wimp won't help her get over her crazy moments and it won't help you to become the kind of man who's impervious to those moments.

Dealing with Her Fears of Abandonment

If a woman had her father walk out on his family when she was younger or she's been emotionally scarred by a heartbreaking break-up or divorce, she may suffer from strong feelings of abandonment. The younger a woman is when she experiences a strong emotional hurt of abandonment the greater it might affect her future relationships. Women like this end up making men jump through endless hoops in order to get them to prove their love and devotion.

A woman who fears abandonment has the capacity to act irrationally hostile towards the man who courts her. Even in an intimate, loving relationship a woman may still struggle with strong feelings of abandonment that compel her to test her man to ensure that he's still "all there" with her.

The sad part about this is that some men believe that by jumping through her hoops they can "prove" themselves to her and earn her loyalty and love. This couldn't be further from the truth. If you've decided that a woman who struggles with a serious fear of abandonment is worth your time (only you will know for sure) you must learn to treat her with tenderness but also with stoutness of heart.

If you want to love her in the way she *needs* you must be willing to set strong boundaries with her and refuse to put up with her drama. If she realizes that you'll put up with any sort of behavior, no matter how damaging it might be to an intimate relationship, she'll keep throwing unnecessary tests your way. She needs to understand that overstepping your personal boundaries has consequences; consequences that you're willing to follow through on should she cross that line with you.

Experiencing a past hurt is not an excuse for on-going suffering. Relationships are meant to be a place of healing and growth. If you failing to set those boundaries that she needs you'll only end up robbing her of the chance to grow into emotional maturity.

She needs to understand that she's more than capable of acting in way that brings satisfaction to both you and her. So no matter how emotional and out of control she gets it is imperative that you stay on course. Don't allow yourself to be swayed in every direction when her fears and insecurities overwhelm her. You can display your empathy because you understand her past but you must be *unafraid* to show her your resolve.

A woman's attraction to you (and your capacity to endure her storms) is dependent upon your ability to be firm but compassionate. Your behavior should not only demonstrate that you will not abandon her, but it should also demonstrate that you won't tolerate her attempts to scare, break, or manipulate you.

Rejecting Her Rejection

Because of her fear of abandonment, a woman might test you to see if you're the kind of man that will "reject her rejection." A woman who has deep insecurities about being rejected or abandoned by men might feel compelled to go out of her way to reject even the most loving, well-meaning man.

You may find that women like this can become very moody all of a sudden and may even struggle with anxiety or depression. For her, the benefit of this test is that it weeds out men who won't be reliable to deal with her brand of personal issues while qualifying men who will love her through and through. It's a defense mechanism that's sure to get her consistent results from the man in her life.

The fear of rejection is a powerful psychological stronghold and it can literally make some women (or men) act in extremely irrational ways. People like this tend to push others away, which make it difficult for them to form and maintain relationships. Because they expect to be rejected they may actually preemptively do and say things to destroy a relationship. At the end of the day it's all really a desperate cry for unconditional love and acceptance.

Women who struggle with this have the underlying limiting belief that *"I will be rejected because of _____."* This belief might be the result of a childhood trauma, guilt, toxic shame, or even a ghost of a relationship gone badly.

Because these beliefs tend to be so powerful, when something happens to overwhelm her emotions, a woman may feel compelled to give you an extremely hard time just to see if you'll bail on her (like she expects you to due to her fear of rejection). If you truly love this woman and you can see her behavior for what it is – an emotional breakdown– you can respond with overwhelming love and reject her rejection.

The men who fail these sorts of tests are the ones who either take it personally or they become angry and insensitive. The trick is not to get caught up in her fears. Instead, stand firm and push through her emotional onslaught until you melt her heart and force her surrender. She will never tell you this, but what she wants is a man who will reject her rejection firmly, ignore her dismissals, embrace her, and affirm her with the loving (or leading) words she desperately needs to hear.

For example, let's say that you just recently married and are getting used to living with one another. A small argument soon leads into a heated fight and she shouts out something like, *"I can't take this anymore. I'm going to sleep by my parents tonight."* An angry, intolerant man may sputter out, *"Fine. See if I care."* Fail. On the other hand, a passive wussy of a man may stutter, *"Please don't leave. Honey, I'm sorry."* This may look good on the surface but what's really going on here?

With that response you are not rejecting her rejection, you're just supplicating her. So what's the best response? Maybe something like, *"No, you're not. THIS is your home now and I want to work through this with you because I love you."* This is the response of a mature, masculine man that loves his wife *with passion* and knows how to reject her rejection.

Of course, you don't want to become an enabler. If she has an emotional issue that compels her to test you consistently you may need to draw the line and call attention to the behavior. A woman with a healthy amount of emotional maturity will be more than willing to work on her issues so that they don't become an overwhelming burden in the relationship.

If her fear of rejection keeps getting the best of her but she tries her best NOT to give you a hard time because of it, you've got yourself a quality woman. On the other hand, if after pointing out the negative patterns of her behavior and she still gives you hell, you may have to utilize more drastic measures (some of them are discussed in this book).

Sometimes you have to be cruel to be kind. It's the responsibility of being a leader. There will be times when a woman needs to be challenged to break out of negative behavioral patterns that have the potential to sabotage a relationship.

Admittedly, women who act this way could be a handful for you if you have little to no experience dealing with people with emotional disorders. Volatile mood swings, debilitating anxiety issues, and depressions are not default characteristics that all women struggle with. So if you're not already highly invested in or married to a woman like this, then take caution when selecting a wife or girlfriend.

CHAPTER 7:
The Single Man and the Women That Test Him

Testing, Dating, and Winning with Women

Author's note: Admittedly, this section applies specifically to single guys as well as guys just getting to know a woman. But you can still gain a lot of insights into female psychology even if you are already married or in a relationship.

If you have just met a woman and you are getting to know her, expect her to test you on various levels. While the intensity of her testing depends on her level of emotional maturity, self-confidence, and general interest in you, it's safe to say that you cannot entirely avoid being challenged in some way.

Don't worry, as you realize by now, getting tested is a good thing. It means a woman is interested in you or wants to be stimulated by you. Read that sentence again.

During the whole process of getting to know you, a woman is going to test you to either amp up the sexual tension, gauge your level of interest (to ensure that you won't hurt her), or to figure out what kind of man you really are on the inside. After she's figured out that she's interested in you, she's going to want to know what your boundaries are and if you're worth her time.

One of the first types of test a woman will use on you is a confidence test and it can come in many forms. Everything from playful teasing, playing hard-to-get, to showing her disapproval for something random about you is a test. She's going to use a number of strategies that's designed to throw you off guard.

If you maintain your frame and keep your head in the game you'll pass with flying colors. If you get angry, get flustered, or find yourself explaining or trying to appeal to her desires – you've lost.

The second type of test you'll come across from a woman you're getting to know is the compliance test. This is a test of your personal boundaries to see how far she can go before you tell her "NO."

For example, let's say you're at a bar and you start chatting her up. Things seem to be going well and all of a sudden, she asks you to buy her a drink. What's really going on here? She's at a bar and I doubt she was dragged there, which means that she came with the understanding that drinks will be on sale and that she'd have to buy one. In other words, she's fully capable of buying her own drinks. This random favor asking is a way to test your willingness to please her. And the more willing you are to please her the less attraction she'll feel for you.

Do not comply with her requests automatically. Engage her on your terms. Lead. If she asks you to buy her a drink, re-frame the exchange in your favor with something like, "I have an even better idea. You buy me a drink you think I'd like and I'll buy you something I think you'll appreciate."

You can even spin it around to implant the idea that she's hitting on you with, "Whoa, slow down. The only women I've ever bought drinks for were all girlfriends. Are you hinting at something?" The message: Don't comply like a wussy and always keep the ball in your court. The only time you should consider a woman's request is if she really does need your gentlemanly help due to an emergency (like a flat tire, etc.).

Boosts to Her Ego

Women get a boost of self-confidence every time they test a man. It's empowering to them, but why? Because no matter what the outcome is they always win.

If a man fails to show his confidence during a test the woman wins because she has successfully weeded out a weak suitor. If a man fails a compliance test a woman now has in her possession a pansy of a man, one who's willing to go that extra mile just to please her. If a man passes a confidence test she has successfully found a gem amongst men. If a man passes a compliance test she has once again, found a man worthy of her time and investment. This is why a woman who learns how to properly test a man cannot lose.

The mere act of testing a man is in and of itself what boosts a woman's confidence. By testing a man she puts herself in the position of the qualifier and this re-framing grants her judicial powers that make most men uncomfortable. By becoming the evaluator she's no longer *as* susceptible to being evaluated by the men around her. It's empowering.

Even the most beautiful women on this planet struggle with a myriad of insecurities, especially when it comes to men. As you interact with her you're probably thinking about how gorgeous she is and in her mind, she's thinking, *"Does he just want my body? Will he lose interest once I start dating him? Is he talking to me because no other woman wants to talk to him?"*

Even though she's insecure and anxious, she's also cunning. Instead of telling you how she's feeling she'll mask her insecurities through challenges designed to make you just as uncomfortable as she might be. The man who remains unfazed while responding in kind with challenges of his own will win her heart.

A woman can be quite in-tune with her hang-ups. She knows that what she really wants is a man to just love her for who she is and that's scary. But for a man to do that she's going to have to be vulnerable with him and trusting of him. As a man passes her tests her trust will increase until her attraction to him outweighs her insecurities. She'll feel overwhelmed with desire and those barriers she's built up to keep you out will melt away. Sounds a lot like falling in love doesn't it? Well, for a lot of women, it is.

Being swept off of her feet by a strong, masculine man is an experience that the women you meet desperately want with a man. Therefore, the man who passes her tests wins her love and more. It's almost as if women know this instinctively, thus the would-be suitor must be tested in order to assess his worth. She wants to *surrender* her all to what she considers a strong, resilient man.

Gauging Her Level of Desire

In the initial phases of dating, one of the prime benefits of learning how to set limits with a woman is that you place yourself in the perfect position to gauge her level of interest in you. If you set a boundary with a woman during the initial phases of dating and she blows up and never wants to see you again, consider yourself a very lucky guy. Things would have never worked out with her in the long-run, and you just saved yourself months of stress and headaches of dealing with a woman who's not compatible with you.

On the other hand, if you set a boundary with her and she sticks around – she's not only obviously VERY interested in you but she also *respects* who you are as a man. The respect she has translates into desire because if she still chooses to continue seeing you, chances are she's become even more attracted to you because of your honesty and self-respect. Setting boundaries and being consistent is vital for filtering out women who have the capacity to submit to your leadership in a relationship and those who cannot.

Some guys tend to think that every interaction with a woman is going to yield them positive results; that no matter who she is, he should always expect to maintain her attraction during the initial dating stages. Reality check: Some women, no matter how hard you try to convince them (or yourself), just won't be that interested in you.

Sometimes it's her, sometimes it is you, but regardless of what went wrong or what went right, a man has to know when to cut his losses and move on. A lot of guys have difficulty cutting their losses when dating women all because of one simple thing – ego.

It's extremely important that you don't allow your ego to cause you to lose your frame with a woman, especially during the initial phases of dating. The minute your ego feels threatened you'll find yourself playing by *her rules* where she's now gauging you to test your level of interest in her. If you learn how to set boundaries with a woman while being more than willing to walk away (especially if she's playing games with you) you will become highly skillful at gauging a woman's level of desire in you.

Sometimes you have to ask yourself how far you're willing to go to "win her heart" or "make her happy." While the idea of romantic love, chivalry, and being a woman's knight-in-shining-armor (Prince Charming) have been ingrained in us since we were old enough to comprehend inter-gender dynamics, it doesn't mean that this model will serve today's modern man effectively when dealing with the fairer sex. If you find yourself repeatedly compromising, adjusting your life to suit her needs and ignoring your own needs and values just to keep her interested in you, you're playing into her game.

While I believe compromise has its place in cultivating relationships, it should be based on win-win solutions rather than win-lose. Only nice guys function on the win-lose plane when dealing with women, and as you already know, you don't want to be Mr. Nice Guy. It's one thing if you're *seducing* the woman you desire, but it's another thing entirely when you find yourself *chasing* her completely on her terms.

While the kind of woman you want to be in a long-term relationship with is one with standards and boundaries of her own, don't fall for the false idea that you should be the only one doing the chasing. If you're constantly chasing a woman, you have no way of measuring her level of desire for you and whether or not she's capable of letting you lead. Read that last sentence again.

The ONLY way you can tell if a woman is comfortable and open to letting you lead her as the man whose authority she can submit to is by setting your own boundaries with her and refusing to engage her on her terms. Be firm in your resolve, assert yourself, and be willing to walk away from a less-than-ideal situation if need be.

For example, let's say that you and a female acquaintance that you're interested in have already suggested that you both should hang out together in the future. Obviously, you both know each other because you share a few mutual friends, and after a bit of on-and-off again light flirting, you're now interested in getting to know her in a more one-on-one setting.

Let's say at some point you decide to give her a call (or text) and tell her that you want to hang out with her at X date, at X time, at X place, just you and her. If she replies back stating that she won't be able to make it but that you both can hang out together with some friends at X date, at X time, and at X place, what we have is a "date" set up on *her terms*.

Now, to the average guy, this all looks well and good. And depending on how bad a guy has it for this girl, he may quickly jump at the chance only to find himself friend-zoned immediately and perhaps indefinitely.

To the naked eye, this seems like a simple change in plans because she may genuinely not be able to make it. She's obviously somewhat interested because she did suggest another "date", albeit with other friends involved. The problem with this situation is, if you don't stick-to-your-guns, you'll never know just how interested she really is.

A woman who's really interested in you (and by interested, I mean "attracted" to you) will jump at the chance to get to know you better in a one-on-one setting. In fact, if she's that interested, she's probably been waiting on you to make a move on her for a while now.

The whole purpose of you setting up a one-on-one meeting with her in the first place was to get to know her personally, without the distraction or buffer of mutual friends. If you deny her social meet up and suggest another one-on-one date only to find that she tries to maneuver it back to a social meet up...have the guts to walk away and say "not interested." Even better, restate your intentions and give her some clarity.

Insist that, "No. I don't want to meet up with friends with you. But I do want to meet you at X place, at X time, on X date. Just the two of us." Only one of two things can happen:

1. She'll realize that you're assertive, know what you want, and are confident enough to walk away from a win-lose situation, which could trigger her attraction for you and make her want to take you up on your offer, or...

2. She'll reject the offer and go about her business being your on-again-off-again light flirting friend of a friend who obviously just likes getting attention from men.

I'll admit, this is a rather simple example, but the principle is sound. Setting boundaries, calling a woman out on her nonsense/games, and sticking to your terms will help you to gauge a woman's level of interest and keep you from wasting your time with flaky, low desire, or low-quality women.

Now, I know all of this sounds pretty heavy, especially if you're just getting to know a woman. I mean, what kind of woman would stick around if a guy just starts throwing his weight around by setting boundaries?

Well, first of all, you're not throwing your weight around. And secondly, we all set boundaries all the time. I've found that in my experiences, and those of others, that in the initial phases of dating women are more likely to test you repeatedly just to see what kind of man are you and if you're worth her future investment.

A quality girl, one who's interested in an assertive, decisive man, is going to have her own boundaries. And whether you like it or not, your ability to start a relationship with her is directly linked to how well you communicate your own boundaries with her and stand by your principles.

When you develop the mindset of a self-assured man, one who knows what he wants and who is comfortable asserting his needs, you'll understand just how necessary boundaries are, even in the simplest of interactions with the opposite sex.

Disagreement Testing for Relationship Suitability

During the dating stages a woman may test you, whether she's consciously or subconsciously aware if it, just to see if you both can "agree to disagree" and still remain attracted to each other. If she figures out that you cannot tolerate disagreements with her, she won't feel confident about your long-term prospects with her.

Disagreements are a natural part of an adult relationship and a quality woman wants to feel assured that you're not going to shut down, shut her out, or blow your top the minute she expresses a divergent point-of-view. This is an important test for a woman to use because when she comes across a man who can stand his ground and still like her, she has a higher chance of enjoying a long-term relationship with effective communication at its foundation. In short, she's testing whether or not you can handle conflict with her and still *want* to be with her in spite of your differences.

Why is it important for a man to know this? It's important because it will help you overcome her tests by not taking her disagreements personally. Sometimes men fail these kinds of tests because of the way they're administered. It reminds me of something that I've reminded female friends about over and over in the past: *When you're communicating with a man, it's not just "what" you say but "how" you say it that matters most to him.*

The trick for women is to learn how to test a man's ability to handle disagreements while not coming off as completely disagreeable or difficult. Whether it's on purpose or not, some women tend to come off a bit untactful and unpleasant as they test men in this way. The problem with this is that it doesn't only cause the guys who can't handle disagreements to walkaway defeated, but it may also cause a quality guy who can actually respectfully disagree to lose his attraction to the woman.

While a quality guy may pass her test by standing his ground and disagreeing respectfully, he may also feel a loss of interest due to way it was handled. This happens because we men enjoy being around women that make us feel more masculine. This has nothing to do with the idea of men having fragile egos or being emotionally weak; it's just a matter of respect.

Remember, the way in which a woman tests you says a lot about who she is. So take into account *how* she disagrees with you. It could mean the difference between passing the tests of an amiable woman that you'll enjoy being around and passing the tests of a disagreeable woman whom you can only tolerate in small doses.

Here's an example of this in action. Let's say that you're discussing a topic of interest with a woman you're getting to know and she disagrees with you. If she phrases her disagreement by saying, *"That doesn't make sense. I don't agree with that at all. I think you're wrong because _____."* Or even worse, she says, *"That's just stupid, and here's why…"*

Obviously, this is a woman who's more interested in being right than building rapport and is in dire need of the book, *How to Win Friends and Influence People*. Granted, in these examples she's not exactly being harsh, but she's not winning any points either.

On the other hand, let's say that she voices her disagreement by saying, *"I disagree with you, but I respect your opinion…"* Or even better, if she understands how men think she might say, *"Personally, I don't agree with you on that, but I'm sure a man like you can handle a little disagreement right?"*

These are simple examples but the takeaway lessons are still effective. Always be aware of the subtext, especially when a woman is testing you. Turn her test into a revealing test of your own.

Don't Lean on a Woman Before It's Time

Leaning on a woman for emotional support and security *before* she has a healthy amount of respect and attraction for you is a sure way to lose her. While opening your heart and being vulnerable with a woman is a great way to build intimacy, it's actually relationship suicide if the proper foundation isn't already in place.

Women require a specific amount of certainty from you before you're "allowed" to show her your more vulnerable side. Women are nurturing and supportive by nature, but that nurturing and support doesn't come for free; it must be earned. A quality woman is more than willing to stand by her man through thick and thin so long as he's already *proven* himself as being worthy of her support.

How does all this apply to being tested by a woman? Well, if you lean on a woman before she's certain of you, in her mind you're actually showing her weakness. If she hasn't already been thoroughly convinced of your strength prior to your vulnerable state, her fear and anxiety will kick in which might compel her to test you. If you signal weakness too early in a relationship, she might feel the need to test you just to make sure that your moment of vulnerability was an isolated incident rather than a habitual part of your make up.

Passing her test will keep her fears in check, which will solidify her confidence in you. Failing her test will confirm her fears (that you're weak and unstable), which will solidify her insecurities and cause her to lose interest in you. In short, leaning on a woman too soon has the potential to backfire on you through a lot of unexpected congruence tests.

I came across a great example of this on a popular dating advice website for women, where the writer openly shared a situation in which she tested a young man who displayed weakness too early.

She stated that in her high school years, a young guy she was interested in opened up to her about how he felt when he approached the casket during his father's funeral. This young man broke down with emotions, complete with sobbing in front of her.

Though she was able to empathize with him to some extent, she admitted that she felt quite alarmed at the young man's display. She saw this young man's weakness too early on in their young relationship, and even worse, she was too young to know how to deal with it.

A few days later, when the young man was back to his normal self, he asked her for a photo of herself as he was so enthralled to have found such a "nice" girl to be with. Desiring to give him a second chance to "prove himself worthy" again after his previous display of "weakness", she decided to test him by making him stay up all night until one of her favorite songs played on the radio. As a reward she would give him the photo he asked for.

Of course, the poor fool took the bait and did what she asked. She lost all attraction for him and dumped him a few days later. Had he called her out on her unreasonable request (or simply waited until she was hooked on him before baring his soul) she wouldn't have given him the boot.

In the early stages of a relationship, some women aren't prepared to deal with all the varieties of a man's inner emotions. Yes, we men have insecurities and we'd love to be with a woman who accepts us the way we are but the ugly truth remains clear: Baring your soul to a woman who's uncertain of your strength and confidence can backfire on you.

Of course, being in an adult relationship requires that we learn to trust our partners fully. I'm not advocating that men should be emotionally hardened and unwilling to be open and vulnerable with their women, all I'm saying is that it's important for men to be a bit more strategic in how they open those doors to their inner emotions. Give her the gift of chipping away at your armor. Give her something to unravel. She'll love you for it.

As I mention in my book, *Attract The Right Girl*, a great way to find out if a woman is long-term relationship material is to observe how she handles you when you're extremely vulnerable. Women with higher levels of emotional maturity and experience in dealing with men are much more able to respond reasonably to isolated moments of masculine weakness than less mature women.

While no woman wants to be with a man who's constantly in emotional turmoil, a more mature woman has the capacity to empathize with her man without labeling him as "weak" during those moments of emotional vulnerability. In fact, if you've been seriously dating a woman for a while and she's seen you at your most emotionally vulnerable, and she still stands by your side and respects you – she's a keeper.

Testing for the Right Woman

If you're only interested in manipulating your way through a woman's tests just to pump-and-dump her you won't like my upcoming advice. Walk away now. On the other hand, if you're interested in seeing how having a low tolerance for tests from women early on can help you attract a high-quality girlfriend, read on.

Now, I purposefully didn't focus on the gamut of congruence tests a woman might throw your way if you're just getting to know her for one very simple reason. An emotionally *mature* woman who's highly interested in you isn't going to go out of her way to be disrespectful or difficult to deal with.

And even if she is highly interested in you but for some reason (lack of emotionally maturity, etc.) acts disrespectfully or difficult with you, why would you want to pursue a relationship with her in the first place? My school of thought is that men looking for quality girlfriends need to develop a high-status mindset in which they are the ones constantly qualifying women not just on beauty alone, but by their inner virtues as well.

After you've already determined that she's physically attractive to you, the biggest factor in determining whether or not she's worth your time is based on how she communicates with you. Naturally, you probably already knew that, but let's take it a step further.

As you're getting to know an attractive woman, don't get caught up with the chemistry alone. A charming woman can create chemistry with you in a heartbeat, but that doesn't guarantee that she's relationship material. What you really want to observe is whether or not she's emotionally mature.

The more emotional maturity a woman has the *less* insecurity and intimidation she'll feel around you. Therefore, she's less likely to throw a ton of tests your way just to make you feel intimidated or insecure. High self-esteem people don't communicate this way, and what you want is a woman with high self-esteem. Of course, if she is attracted to you she will feel butterflies and nervousness just like anyone else, but that doesn't mean she'll use that as an excuse to be manipulative or excessively difficult.

Be Open but Be Honest

Let's say you're just getting to know a woman and in an attempt to find a meaningful connection you share yourself with her quite openly. As you converse with her in this way you notice that she starts testing you in a way that's clearly disrespectful or in bad taste. You clearly don't have any kind of established relationship with this woman but she's giving you a hard time anyway. What's the deal?

Now, just because she's interested in you (since she's testing you and all) doesn't mean you should just accept it and roll with the punches. If during your interactions with her she *repeatedly* displays behaviors that scream "crazy chick", "drama queen", or "manipulative brat", walk away.

Sure you can play her game, tease, and outwit her in an attempt to make a connection and build "attraction", but at what cost? Acting in this way lowers your standards by default thus ensuring that you'll continue to attract these types of women. By setting strong boundaries and having standards you'll project out into the world that you know what you want and that you're more than willing to walk away from an unfavorable situation.

Manipulative men and "nice" guys don't do this. Manipulative men attract drama queens because they can relate to them on that level. Nice guys attract drama queens, gold diggers, and domineering women because they don't have strong boundaries at all.

Learning how to outwit a woman who insists on putting you through the ringer from the start is a waste of time if you're interested in finding the right girl. If you have higher standards for what you want to *experience* with a woman you're far more likely to attract the kind of quality woman who also wants the same thing. You won't attract what you want, you'll attract that which you are.

Not All Women "Want" to Play Games

If you call a woman out on her behavior and she apologizes and chooses to play nice, then good. If she defends herself or continues in her negative behavior even after you've drawn attention to it, look at the situation for what it is – a waste of your time and hers.

In this case, when it comes to your values and emotional needs you both are clearly mismatched. You therefore have no need to play her games just to create a relationship.

By being honest with your preferences you're sure to come across women who *will* perceive you as over-sensitive, straight-laced, or even no fun at all. Who cares? These sorts of women weren't right for you to begin with so why should their opinion of you matter at all? Most men think that they need to "win" in every situation with every woman they come across. That's a stupid way to look at dating.

If what you really seek is a meaningful connection with a woman who's highly attracted to you and vice versa, be willing to walk away from the emotionally immature ones. You do this by knowing what you want and not giving two cents about what a woman thinks about you.

The more cutthroat you are with this the less experiences you'll have with manipulative drama queens who insist on giving you a hard time. I'm not saying it'll be easy but it's definitely worth it. All women test men, yes, but not all women play mind games. There are gorgeous high-quality women out there that want to date men who desire meaningful connections rather than manipulative game playing.

Your dating life will become much more abundant once you adopt this way of thinking. You'll burn less mental energy trying to verbally out maneuver women, which makes it easier for you to connect with women who meet your standards. If more men would just say, *"I'm no longer interested. I don't like your attitude, it's atrocious"* most guys wouldn't find themselves stuck with drama queen wives and girlfriends.

Leave Her in Better Shape Than You Found Her

You may have heard it said that as a gentleman, it's better to leave a woman better than you found her. Well, this idea also applies to her own awareness of how her behavior, good or bad, affects the men she relates with.

If you've been dating a woman who's in desperate need of an attitude adjustment and you know without a shadow of a doubt that you've had as much as you can tolerate from her, for heaven's sake, please make things easier for the next guy she dates BEFORE you move on.

What I mean is, don't blow her off or break up with her before you take the time to set her straight. Do your brethren a solid and call her out on her negative behavior before you put her back out there on the dating market. If you just tolerate her negative behavior and disrespect without saying anything you're doing a disservice to the rest of your fellow men and her as well. You should leave her better off, or at least more knowledgeable, than you found her.

Here's an example of this at work in another area of life. If you're fired from three different jobs within a six-month time period and none of your old employers ever took the time to tell you why, they're doing both you and your future employers a disservice.

Why is it a disservice? Because you won't ever know the behaviors or attitudes that make such a useless or low-quality employee and your future employers will now have the pleasure of finding out just how unfit of an employee you are for themselves; wasting both your time and theirs.

If your first employer had the *compassion* (be cruel to be kind) to tell you the truth about yourself maybe you would have changed your ways and would have been able to keep your second job. But since no one told you the cold, hard truth, you never became aware of the problem and therefore never had the opportunity to make a change for the better.

I use the little example above to convey the idea that it's better for you to call a woman out on her negative behavior than to just let her get on with her life. Give her the opportunity to change by making her aware of her behavior and how it has the potential to ruin her relationships with men.

I'm not espousing that you act like her father, but at least be man enough to express your dissatisfaction. It's better to set her straight and then move on with your life than call it quits while she lives in ignorance, ready to burden some other poor fellow with her wild and immature ways.

Complaining to your friends in a bar that she was a rude, spoiled, disrespectful drama queen, etc. right after dumping her or blowing her off without some attempt on your part to express your discontent is the easy way out. Be a man and call her out on her foolishness, then, without hesitation, let her go and move on. If you mattered to her even in the slightest I guarantee the blow to her ego will be felt and she might even consider taking the introspective journey of self-improvement.

If she realizes the error in her ways she'll respect you for calling her out and might even beg for a second chance. But even more important is the fact that you'll have expressed your personal boundaries to her and your willingness to walk away – things that increase your value as a man.

Yes, it's true. Just like men, some women won't learn right away. That's not your job. Your job is to at least say something to increase her awareness. Think of it as constructive criticism. If other wimpy men come along who tolerate her bad behavior enough to pursue a relationship with her after you've moved on, that's no sweat off your back. You did your part and became a better man for it.

I believe that if more men had the guts to set women straight instead of just moving on in silence, you'd find less men stuck in relationships with domineering, manipulative, drama queens.

CHAPTER 8:
Building a Better Man

Do You Have the Right to Lead Her?

A good friend of mine once told me a story of how he was rejected by an attractive girl that he was interested in. The interesting part was that she was crying and obviously hurt by someone, but when he attempted to console her, her reaction to him was cold, mean, and frankly…insulting.

When he explained this tale to me, I couldn't help but wonder about the implications. Naturally, he went into a lot more detail than I just did, so I was able to analyze the situation quite in depth with him. And after a few moments of questioning and pontification, we arrived at a very simple reason why his offering of comfort was a complete turn off for her. It's simple: *he didn't have the RIGHT to comfort her.*

Before you can lead a woman, she's going to have to have some sort of trust in you. My friend, though his intentions were sincere (even though he would have used her misfortune to build rapport with her), was not the kind of man she could trust, at least not at the time of the incident. He was weak, needy, and definitely an average frustrated chump, and she knew it. Even in her compromised position she would not allow herself to be comforted by a man who lacked the strength she craved. In short, she probably felt that he had no right (authority) to comfort her in her time of need.

Standing up to a difficult woman requires being authoritative. If she's giving you the business, you need to be able to assert your personal boundaries naturally. A woman with a bit of experience in dealing with men isn't going to be fooled by a one or two time occurrence.

Even after you begin standing up to her, she's going to test you, over and over again to ensure that the one time you finally defended your personal boundaries wasn't a one off. She needs consistency from you, the type of consistency that can only come from a man who has not only learned how to *exercise* his authority in a relationship but he's also learned how to *be* an assertive man.

Being assertive to your core means that your behavior is influenced by your mindset. You're not reliant merely on techniques. Instead, because of your decisive, principle-led nature, you play the part *naturally* without much thought. This is what your woman is going to be looking for, because without consistent displays of assertiveness on your part, she's not going to be convinced by your once-every-now-and-then acts of authority.

As you've probably realized by now, what she wants is *congruence* from the man in her life. And the best way to ensure that you're on top of your game more often than not is to move past the point of just *acting* alpha and focus your energy on *becoming* a strong, self-assured man at your core instead.

Give Up Your Need for Coddling

In the event you don't know the definition of "coddle", it is to treat in an indulgent or overprotective way. That means that if you're a man who needs coddling, especially from women, then in order for you to feel secure about yourself you must be treated in an indulgent or overprotective way.

I remember being in junior high and I was definitely having one of those days where things just weren't going my way. In Biology class, I had this female teacher that insisted on giving the guys in our class a hard time. She was a new teacher, and looking back I realize that what she was actually doing was testing to see which guys she had absolute authority over in our class and which of them would be more likely to give her a hard time.

On the day in question, she said something that was particularly insulting to me, in front of the entire class. I felt hurt and embarrassed and it showed. It was quite evident that she had "hurt my feelings" and she came over, put her arm around me and apologized. Yes, this actually happened in junior high school, in front of EVERYONE. Believe me, I'm cringing as I write this.

So why do I bring up this dark, painful, unmanly memory that I swore to take to my grave? Well, all for your benefit. In this little tidbit from my past, it was obvious that I needed coddling. From that moment on, she watched what she said to me not out of respect but out of pity. I got what I wanted, which was to be left alone, but it wasn't because she respected me.

My sensitivity shone through quite easily, and the other kids in the class didn't feel the same kind of pity for me, I can tell you that much. I'm almost sure that that one event caused a whole lot of junior high school suffering that took me awhile to correct.

Looking back, what I should have done was to have an adult-like "cease and desist" conversation with her at that moment or respond with cockiness and humor. Since she was so willing to "go there" with me I should have had the guts to do the same with her. Unfortunately, I didn't, and it will forever be a lesson learned of how *not* to respond to unwanted jests or a woman's tests.

The Right Attitude

When it comes to passing a woman's tests or putting her in her place it is not always what you say that matters most, once again it's *how* you say it. When a woman steps out of line with you or does something you think is below her, you don't have to be rude, whiny, or angry to state your displeasure or disapproval. You don't have to be aggressive; neither do you have to sulk to express your opinions. Act like an adult male.

I honestly feel that handling these sorts of situations must be done with tact, firmness, and a sincere concern for her well-being. In other words, maintain the position of the leader she expects you to be but let your actions come from a place of love.

Think of it along the lines of a father. You love your children but you have to do and say things they won't like because you have their best interests at heart. You're not concerned about what your child thinks of you during the time of punishment. You're more concerned about their well-being, now and in the future. You choose to be the "bad guy" sometimes because it's the right thing to do. And most importantly, you're always fair and honest with your judgments, no matter how unpopular they may be.

Men Who Care Too Much

Can you confidently stand on stage and deliver a speech about something you believe in in front of an angry crowd of thousands of women who vehemently disagree with everything you have to say? It's okay if you said, "no." Not many men can.

Why? Well, if we take out the fear of public speaking it could simply be due to the fear of having an unpopular opinion. It could even be due to the fear of disapproval and rejection, especially by women. It could be due to the fear of being criticized and ostracized by women. Or it could be because of all these things in combination.

So what's my point? Nice guys, male doormats, and conflict-avoidant men are petrified of being "misunderstood" or disliked, especially by women. They care too much about what people think of them and place their self-worth into the hands of the crowd. And in this case, it's a crowd of women.

It's absolutely intolerable for a woman to be upset at them, think negatively of them, or to feel utter contempt for them. Men like this will do just about anything to avoid confrontational situations with women just to prevent the intense feelings of discomfort that come with it.

While it is important for men to be mindful of how they are perceived by their honor group (group of male friends, male mentors, etc.), it doesn't benefit them the same way when it comes to the opposite sex. Becoming indifferent to what a woman might think of you when you act based on your principles is one of the most powerful attitude shifts you can make as a man. The benefits to your overall well-being will astound you, as will the positive effect it has on *how* you experience a woman's tests. When you're not trying to read her mind to see whether or not she'll approve of what you have to say, you have greater freedom to act from a place of integrity.

Hyper-analyzing what a woman might think, say, do, or feel if you behaved a certain way causes intense anxiety. Over time, such anxiety turns into fear. The kind of fear that causes you to hem, haw, and second guess every decision you *want* to make. It's not a pretty picture to observe a man trapped in a cage of his own making as he hands over the sanctity of his own mind to a woman.

How This Behavior Plays Out

This sort of behavior plays out in all the usual ways that people-pleasers display. Sometimes it's subtle; other times it's not so subtle, but it always shows itself in how a man interacts with a woman. Here's a short list of what these behaviors look like:

- Editing your choice of words or pussyfooting with your diction so as not to displease or arouse a woman's anger in any way.

- Making tentative suggestions to gain her approval instead of making clear statements. For example: *"Honey, I'm thinking we should eat Chinese tonight."* This is a suggestion and you're clearly waiting for her approval.

- Censoring your opinions, behavior, and even your own needs just to keep her happy and unprovoked.

- Thinking excessively about what she'll think, say, or do if you say or do what you want to do.

- Trying to be perfect to earn the approval of others.

It's not easy to admit that you've become a whipped shell-of-a-man. And it's even harder to change what could be years of passive, people-pleasing habits that have now defined your relationships. It is time for a change, a change in your self-beliefs that can redefine your relationships.

Redefine Your Self-Worth

A man's self-worth should not be inextricably linked to the health of his romantic relationship. Imagine how horrible it must be if the value you place on yourself as a man is one hundred percent *dependent* on whether or not things are going well with you and your woman.

Some men won't admit this, but because they place such a high level of value on their ability to "make a woman happy" the moment their wives or girlfriends become unhappy with them (or even unhappy in general) they lose their sense of self-worth. It's as if men like this suffer from a limiting belief, one that equates their personal value with the value of their relationship. Once the relationship falters so does everything else in their lives.

This perpetual dependency has the capacity to immobilize them should the woman they love show any sign of discord. This is a preposterously flawed paradigm to live. No man should place a major portion of his well-being on his significant other's approval and agreeability.

The limiting belief that the level of perfection in a relationship equates to one's self-worth can manifest itself in other ways as well. Some men, in combination with their need to please others may link their self-worth to how healthy their relationship appears to the outside world.

In their eternal quest for approval, they'd rather hide the defects of their relationship in order to maintain the illusion of perfection and/or superiority. But little do they know that they're not fooling anyone. The moment someone speaks negatively of their relationship they become self-doubting and visibly insecure. The moment someone speaks positively about their relationship they burst with seeming confidence and aplomb.

I speak of such things not from a soapbox, but from my own humbling experiences. A particular example from my own life comes to mind. My wife and I were once invited to play a couples' game called Spouse-o-logy along with three other couples. It's a game that tests your knowledge of your spouse, kind of like *The Newlywed Game* television show. At first the game started off quite fun, but as it progressed I soon began to seethe with frustration.

We were losing. Horribly.

To make matters worse I couldn't figure out why the Dickens I was getting so worked up. As the game went on I grew less and less enthused about playing which solidified our spectacular loss against the other married couples. It was not one of my proudest moments, I can tell you that much.

Now, I am a very introspective person and upon deep pontification the following day I slowly realized why I had lost my cool and taken our defeat so personally. I realized that I had so much of my own self-worth tied to *what the other couples thought of my marriage* that I couldn't stand to lose at such a game. Ridiculous, I know, but don't judge me.

I realized that I couldn't believe that my wife and I were losing to the other couples. Weren't we perfect, or at least superior to the other couples? How dare we get those questions wrong in front of our friends and thereby remove the illusory veil of ostensible perfection.

Granted, I did take into consideration that I can be hyper-competitive when it comes to knowledge-based games (it's a writer thing). I also admit that I HATE losing, perhaps even on a cellular level. But even with those considerations I grasped that something was very off about my attitude towards the whole thing.

I took the loss far too personally and this was BEFORE we were even mid-way through the game. It wasn't logical, and therefore I deduced that my own inner beliefs about *how we looked to others as a couple* caused the unnecessary frustration. The challenge thereon out was to redefine my self-worth by becoming more down-to-earth. I needed to give up my need to have others bear witness to my "perfect" marriage, and I also needed to simply lighten up.

It's important for a man to learn from his experiences, no matter how painful, embarrassing, or humbling they may be. This was definitely one of the more humbling experiences and it taught me a great deal of some of my own inner struggles at the time.

Not taking yourself so seriously helps a great deal to keep your head out of your behind. Besides, in retrospect, no one cared that we were losing. Each couple evidently had their own issues; issues that they laughed about together and took in stride. Lesson learned, and I'm a better man for it.

Developing a Strong Frame

As a man, one of the most powerful concepts I've learned is the idea of *framing*, the awareness that the most sacred thing about a man is the integrity of his own mind. It's the notion that a man must have such a strong conviction of his core values that nothing in his external environment can shake him of his self-belief or remove him from his path. This is the power of a man who has full possession of his own mind.

The great, American philosopher, Ralph Waldo Emerson, wrote a powerful essay called, *Self-Reliance*. The following is a short passage from this essay that sums up the idea of framing and how important it is for a man to be free from the opinions of others:

"What I must do is all that concerns me, not what the people think. This rule, equally arduous in actual and in intellectual life, may serve for the whole distinction between greatness and meanness. It is the harder because you will always find those who think they know what is your duty better than you know it. It is easy in the world to live after the world's opinion; it is easy in solitude to live after our own; but the great man is he who in the midst of the crowd keeps with perfect sweetness the independence of solitude."

Of course, we can get deep into a philosophical discussion about the importance of not being so bullheaded and stuck in our thinking that we have difficulty gaining the support of others to truly make a difference in the world. But we won't. I used this quote because it serves the idea of 'framing' perfectly in that it's better to avoid being a *slave* to the opinions of others so that you can *choose* outside advice and knowledge much more freely.

What you think and believe about yourself, your life, your loved ones, your career, etc. should have more value to you than how everyone else views it. Passing a woman's tests requires a self-approved frame of mind; therefore, being <u>dependent</u> on outside opinions will only lead to failure. You cannot lead a woman, or anyone else for that matter, if you crave being popular.

To have a rock-solid, masculine frame is to commit to who you are, knowing that you're unwilling to sacrifice who you are just to make someone else happy. Men without a strong frame may find that they often change their opinions and behaviors around different groups of people. They are chameleons that usually aren't sure of who they are regardless of how confident they may *pretend* to be on the outside. Men like this struggle the most not only with being tested by women, but being tested by life in general.

Here's a simple example of a man maintaining his frame with his buddy:

Let's say you were going to the movies and a good friend arrived to pick you up. It's a late showing and you decide to throw on a cap because you just love how caps look on you. Your buddy arrives, glances at you for a moment, raises an eyebrow, and asks, *"You're wearing a hat?"* The subtext behind his questioning is, *"Dude, there's no sun in the movie theater. You'll look silly. Take it off and let's go."*

A man with a weak frame might try to explain his choice of apparel. He may even feel silly and take it off. A man with a strong frame, who's fully convinced of his sense of style, might say something like, *"And you're not?"* Boom. He re-framed the exchange to illustrate that he's confident with his choice, he doesn't care what anyone thinks, and most importantly, that he's somewhat baffled as to why his friend wouldn't wear one as well.

Men with strong frames look on the inside to see if they're on the right path. They often look at the outside world wondering why more people aren't doing it the way they are. Men with weak frames do just the opposite. They are always looking on the outside as they try to do things as right and perfect as they can. And when they do look inward all they see are the mistakes they're making and the things that need fixing.

Don't do this. I can tell you from personal experience that this is no way for a man to live his life. So do yourself a favor and stop living in a perpetual cycle of self-doubt. It's unmanly.

Do you now see the dangers to your relationships and the anxiety-inducing stress that can come from having a weak frame as a man? Good, because so do women. And they will test the living daylights out of you until you figure out who you are as a man and confidently *assert* those inner convictions.

Resist the impulse to torture yourself by caring too much about what other people think of you. It's a habit of thought, a type of mental conditioning, and just like any other habit it can be unlearned over time.

Power Comes from Living by Principles

Your masculine confidence and ability to lead a woman must come from a place of authenticity or else she won't believe it. She won't buy what you're selling if she can sense that you're just putting on a show. While you can fake it for a while, she'll continue to test you until you break.

Therefore, the only way to avoid succumbing to her challenges is to ensure that your leadership comes from a place of inner conviction. In other words, you must be the kind of man that stands on principle.

When it's all said and done, a man is nothing without his principles and values. This is the essence of true manliness, the core of masculine maturity; the very thing that high-quality women desperately crave from their men.

When what a man says and does matches his internal beliefs, he maintains a high self-esteem. When his words and actions betray what he truly believes, he loses respect for himself due to his lack of congruency (there's that word again). The man who lives by unbending principles will not feel threatened by the ideas and opinions of others. Read that again.

Great men who have provided the greatest services to mankind all have one thing in common. They built their lives on the unchanging principles of life itself. We know these men as being men of high-character, greatly magnanimous, and full of virtue. And it is this fullness of virtue that makes a man impervious to the ever-changing world around him.

A woman pushes and smashes against you with her storms of emotions to test this very foundation. She wants to know if the man standing before her is made of sand or is he made of stone. She asks herself, *"Can he be counted on to do the right thing or will he crumble just to appease me?"*

Eventually, as a man becomes truly led by his principles he will grow to find her tests amusing, her challenges will merely seem like a byproduct of her feminine wiles, and her pesky longings for him as affirmations of her loyalty. In short, he will have mastered her femininity not by controlling her, but by fortifying his own masculinity.

Men with high self-esteem, those who exude masculine confidence, don't live by what others think is best for them. The core of their decision-making isn't driven by what the boss wants, what the wife wants, what the kids want, what the clergyman wants, or what their friends want. No. These men are driven by their principles.

If a man's principles dictate that he must speak the truth, he will not lie to appease his superiors at work. Living by his principle – speaking truthfully – is more important to him than whether or not his boss likes him. If a man's principles dictate that he must spend some time each day working diligently on his goals, he's less likely to spend the entire day engaged in slothful activity. However, if he does find himself wasting time he'll soon feel a little nagging sensation in the back of his conscience until he straightens up and flies right.

A man's principles are like streetlights that guide him along the dark, narrow paths of life. Whenever he gets lost or loses track, as we all do from time to time, they serve as markers to lead him back towards the straight and narrow.

On the other hand, if a man's decision making is centered on producing a profit at all cost he's likely to do questionable things in order to achieve his ends. Hence why many businesses partake in morally questionable practices today. They're driven not by moral principles but by competition, profit, keeping employees happy, and expediency.

Principles keep a man centered even as the world about him falls into absolute chaos. He remains intact and unbending to circumstance because he has, in fact, built his life on unchanging truths.

Consider for a moment that a man's body may decay over time and even his wealth can disappear overnight, but no one event can easily destroy a man's character. In fact, the reverse is true. Where time and conflict can destroy a man's body and even rob him of his wealth, if a man stands by his principles, such things will only serve to strengthen his character. A man's inner strength comes from living by principle.

A man decides on his principles as he meditates on his personal path. After considering what he wants out of life he'll be able to confidently choose his core values and the principles he wants to align himself with.

Many remarkable books have been written to help men with this process of self-discovery. One of the best ones I've already mentioned in an earlier chapter. *<u>The 7 Habits of Highly Effective People</u>*, by author Stephen Covey, does a great job at helping the reader figure out what's truly important to them in life and how to go about prioritizing one's activities in order to live both by principle and one's own core values. I highly recommended you digest this book if you have trouble making decisions based on your principles.

Women Treat You How You Treat You

We always earn what we *believe* we deserve even if we *think* we deserve better. Therefore, even a woman will treat you how you *allow* and *train* her to based on your own self-belief. Understanding this one concept is the starting point to becoming a man with strong personal boundaries. Because your reality is a perpetual and often merciless mirror of what you believe about yourself, you'll never be able to change the way a woman treats you if you don't believe that you deserve better.

The human mind functions in such a way as to attain congruence (there's that word again). It will work overtime to close the gap between who you think you are and what your behaviors portray until the two correspond. This is why you're compelled to behave in a way that matches with your self-belief. As the saying goes, *"you can't hide what's inside."*

If you inwardly believe that you're a man of low-value, just about everyone you relate with will treat you as such. Even your adoring wife or girlfriend might find herself struggling to treat you with respect if you neglect your own well being over time. No woman wants to be with a loser (unless she's a loser herself) and she'll give a man hell in an effort to induce a positive change.

So, what's the solution? How does a man increase his sense of self-worth and make it difficult for anyone to disrespect him? How does a man ensure that the opinion he has of himself is worth more to him than the opinions of others? The answer is so simple it's embarrassing to say: Develop rock-solid self-belief by becoming a better man.

If You Build It, She Will Come Around

You cannot force a woman to change her behavior towards you but you can make it difficult and even hazardous for her to treat you with disrespect simply by taking control of your personal growth. By focusing on becoming a high character, high quality man who has immense social value, a wise woman would think twice before going out of her way to make your life a living hell.

A woman wants a man who will remain steadfast on his path towards masculine maturity. And as long as he's passionately committed to his path and ensuring that she remains a part of that journey, she'll have little reason to spur him into action through a hell storm of congruence and commitment tests.

It's difficult to disrespect a man who after twenty years of marriage, is still in shape, his kids are well-behaved, has a wildly successful career/business, and has a gorgeous wife who is still sexually interested in and loyal to him. Of course, no one's life is usually this perfect all the time, but that doesn't mean a man shouldn't at least make a strong *attempt* to get in shape, keep his home in order, and secure his family's financial future all while leading and loving his wife with passion.

Because women are hard-wired to seek out and secure the love and loyalty of a man who leads, you're going to have to up your game if you want a woman to respect, desire, and submit to your authority. While there may be physically fit guys with great careers who just need to work on setting better boundaries with their wives and girlfriends, other guys who struggle with being disrespected by women tend to be lacking in other very important areas.

These are *highly* important aspects of a man's life that have a great effect on his overall well-being. It's usually when a man comes up lacking in these areas that a woman determines that he doesn't possess enough "value" to her. Sometimes by getting his life in order a man finds that his problems with women tend to take care of themselves.

If your girlfriend has been financially supporting you for the past two years and she suddenly has the audacity to speak to you how she wants…it's kind of obvious what your *real* problem is. If you've been packing on the pounds for the last five years while after two kids your wife is in better shape than she's been in decades, yet she has the nerve to withhold sex from such a loyal husband such as yourself, it should be obvious what's *really* going on.

Sarcasm aside, these are all serious situations because some men don't seem to have a clue why a woman would treat them with utter contempt even though they *think* they're being the kind of man women would kill for.

Make no mistake; I'm not claiming that slacking off in one area of your life is grounds for a woman to act disrespectfully towards you. But if she's been carrying your load, handling your responsibilities, or simply outclassing you for quite some time, eventually this imbalance will compel her to force you into action so that she's not forced to take her business elsewhere.

I know, it's ugly, and life isn't fair. If you want, after you finish this book you're welcome to purchase many of the thousands of books available out there that will make you *feel* better with sweet, sweet lies.

Again…sarcasm.

The path to become a better man implies that you're investing in yourself in order to increase your overall well-being and your value to the world. You'll find that by doing so you cannot help but treat yourself with much greater respect, which increases your self-esteem and confidence.

As this confidence radiates out into the world you'll find yourself no longer settling for disrespectful behavior from either men or women. A man with high value has options and he'd rather walk away from an unfavorable situation then play the part of the victim. As you become a better man you'll realize that you actually *deserve* better, and you'll expect it.

In reality, a man who remains stagnate with his personal growth will continue to face major difficulties with the woman who is emotionally invested in him. What we have in this case is a man with a structural problem when it comes to his masculine strength and confidence. A man facing a structural problem like this can only change his situation by taking bold, consistent action. Therefore, if you've fallen into a rut with your own masculine maturation, consider taking action on many of the character strengthening activities I suggest in my other book, *What Women Want In A Man*.

The Conclusion

The purpose of this book wasn't to turn you into a club-wielding caveman; it was to bring some balance back to your masculinity. The only time you'll really need to "put your foot down" or "show some backbone" with a woman is if she's overstepping your boundaries, being unreasonable, or trying to control you in any way. And although men should lead in their relationships, that doesn't mean that women want to be pushed around. While women don't want to be bossed around, they want to know that you won't allow them to boss you around either.

I honestly feel that in a relationship, when a man understands why and how his woman tests him he will be able to love her all the more and even unconditionally. As human beings we tend to demonize that which we don't understand. If you don't understand why your woman tests you it's easy to take things personally when she does test you which leads to your resentment and anger. If you don't understand how your woman tests you, you may end up reacting negatively to her, which causes her to feel anger and resentment instead.

Understanding this unique facet of the feminine experience will not only transform you into a relationship Jedi but it will help you to forgive your wife or girlfriend much more readily, even when she says or does something to elicit a negative emotional response from you.

So, what's the moral of the story? Be strong, be confident, tease her playfully, and most importantly…lead her. Don't shirk your role as a man, don't default your responsibilities to women, don't seek her approval, and don't be predictable. When she loses herself in her emotions you *must* maintain your frame, stay your course, and refuse to hand over your balls. In short, don't be a pushover.

Let her emotions wash over you like a crashing wave against an immovable rock. If you can look her hostility in the eye, peer deep into the chaos of her insecurities, and stand firm through the storms of her emotions, you're doing better than most men.

It all comes down to really empathizing with a woman and giving her what she *needs* and not necessarily what she wants in that moment. This is something that comes from experience. The more time you spend with a woman the more you learn about her inner needs and uncontrollable desires.

Once you maintain your frame of controlled power, no matter what she throws your way you'll be able to see through the charade and meet her deepest needs. Remember, in order for a man to fully love a woman he must overcome his fear of her emotions.

No matter how many relationship books you read, how many books on being romantic or attracting women you study, you will always arrive at the same conclusion over and over again. And it's this…

Women want to be loved by a man who leads. Any effort to seduce her or win her heart with romance will only backfire if she doesn't already respect you as a man.

I just gave you the best piece of advice you'll find

about women. So, burn that sentence onto your memory before you finish this book.

Before you go...

I just wanted to say, "thank you" for purchasing my book.

I know you could have picked from dozens of books on understanding women, but you took a chance on my guide and for that I'm extremely grateful. So, thanks again for purchasing this book and reading all the way to the end.

Now, if you liked this book, **please take a minute or two to leave a review for it on Amazon so that other men just like you can find out more about it**. Your feedback is most appreciated as it helps me to continue writing books that get you results.

And "thank you" in advance for your review. I am eternally grateful.

Men's Books by Bruce Bryans:

Below is a list of my other books for men that you can find on Amazon.com. You can easily find them all here at: http://www.amazon.com/author/brucebryans

***

What Women Want In A Man: How to Become the Alpha Male Women Respect, Desire, and Want to Submit To

In *What Women Want In A Man*, you'll learn how to become a high-quality, self-confident man that can naturally attract a good woman, maintain her sexual attraction to you, and keep her "well-behaved" in a relationship.

What Women Want When They Test Men: How to Decode Female Behavior, Pass a Woman's Tests, and Attract Women Through Authenticity

In *What Women Want When They Test Men*, you'll learn how to recognize and pass a woman's tests and become the assertive man that can maintain a woman's respect, sexual interest, and unwavering support.

Attract The Right Girl: How to Find Your Dream Girl and Be the Man She Can't Resist

In *Attract The Right Girl*, you'll discover how to find and choose an amazing girlfriend (who's perfect for you) and how to spark the kind of attraction that'll lead to a long-term relationship with her.

How To Be A Better Boyfriend: The Relationship Manual for Becoming Mr. Right and Making a Woman Happy

In *How To Be A Better Boyfriend*, you'll discover how to cultivate a more fun, satisfying, and easy-going relationship with your dream girl, and what to do to avoid all the drama, bad girlfriend behavior, and game playing that many "nice guys" often fall prey to in relationships.

Meet Her To Keep Her: The 10 Biggest Mistakes That Prevent Most Guys from Attracting and KEEPING an Amazing Girlfriend

In *Meet Her To Keep Her*, you'll learn the ten dating mistakes that stop most guys from attracting and keeping a 'Total 10 girlfriend' and how to overcome them.

Find Your Path: A Short Guide to Living with Purpose and Being Your Own Man...No Matter What People Think

In *Find Your Path*, you'll discover how to find your mission in life and how to become a much more self-assured man of purpose and inner conviction.

About Bruce Bryans

Bruce Bryans is a successful author with a passion for research into the dating and mating rituals of men and women. He doesn't fashion himself as some all-knowing "relationship guru", but instead prefers to provide insightful information based on the social and biological factors that bring men and women together for love and romance. Bruce has written numerous books on topics including: masculinity, attraction, dating strategy, and gender dynamics within romantic relationships. Bruce's main aim is to provide easy-to-implement, practical information that helps men and women improve their dating market value and mating desirability to the opposite sex.

When he isn't tucked away in some corner writing a literary masterpiece (or so he thinks), Bruce spends most of his time engaged in manly hobbies, spending time with friends, or being a lovable nuisance to his wife and children.

You can learn more about his writings and receive updates (and future discounts) on his books by visiting his website at: www.BruceBryans.com

Share the Wisdom

If you've been enlightened, inspired, or helped in any way by this book, please recommend it to your brothers, sons, co-workers, and friends. If you're a blogger or fellow author, consider recommending it to your readers. And if you're a dating coach, therapist, counselor, etc., and you strongly believe that this book can help your clients, please consider recommending it to them or purchasing copies to give away as gifts.

I sincerely hope that this book has given you greater insight into women and attraction, and I hope it will inspire you to inspire other men as well.

Here's to your success!

Bruce Bryans

Printed in Great Britain
by Amazon